A NOTE ON THE AUTHOR

Barry Fantoni was born in the East End of London in 1940 to an Italian father and a Jewish mother of French and Dutch extraction, both of whom were gifted musicians. In 1963, following a period of travel and a sell-out one-man show in London, Fantoni joined *Private Eye* as a member of the editorial staff. His work appeared in all but thirty-one issues of the magazine over fifty years. In 1966 he was given the job of creating and presenting a TV show exploring popular trends in the arts called *A Whole Scene Going*. Fantoni now lives in Turin where he writes books, plays, poetry and screenplays.

A Whole Scene Going On

A Whole Scene Going On

The Inside Story of *Private Eye*, the Pop Revolution and London in the Swinging Sixties

BARRY FANTONI

For Katie and Mr Watson

First published in Great Britain in 2019 by Polygon, an imprint of Birlinn Ltd,
West Newington House, 10 Newington Road, Edinburgh EH9 1QS

www.polygonbooks.co.uk

1

ISBN 978 1 84697 489 2

British Library Cataloguing-in-Publication Data
A catalogue record for this book is available on request from the British Library.

Design and typesetting by Studio Monachino

CONTENTS

PREFACE

This memoir is what it says. A book of Sixties memories. It is not a social history. Half a century later, the facts may not be as clear as I remember them, or in the right order. But that is the case with everything remembered. Nothing is precise, no matter how hard we try to make it so. Even what we did last week can often cause more than a moment's reflection: was it Wednesday or Thursday I went to the osteopath? Some things are more vivid than others. I have never been sure where to place the line between what I remember and what I imagine. I sometimes suspect there isn't one.

From 1960 until 1973 I lived and worked in a studio overlooking Clapham Common. The door was open to all. Some who walked into my studio were famous. Others not. But all of them were part of the Sixties revolution. Paul, Ray, Pete, Marianne, Cook and Angela, the girl next door. All of them. Inventive, open-minded and brilliant people who created a unique decade with an openness to new ideas that had not been seen before, nor seen since.

My book is about these people and is dedicated to them. No one can bring about a people's revolution alone and the Sixties was such a revolution, one in which I played a very small but very large part. (You're fired, ed.) I would add that there were many others who helped shape the Sixties, some as much or more than those I have written about. People like Joan Littlewood and her theatre at Stratford East. And dress designer Barbara Hulanicki who started Biba. Mike Hodges and his mould-breaking art programme *Tempo*. Not forgetting the most unpleasant man I have ever met, multi-millionaire hit-maker Mickie Most. Sadly there has to be a limit. After all, this book is not *Remembrance of Things Past*. It is only lack of space that has caused their contributions to be omitted.

My dear Italian dad used to boast to strangers that, in 1935, Mussolini asked him to paint his portrait. His story was very convincing. Crammed with details about what wine they drank and the size of the canvas. It was to be a full-size portrait in full uniform. I think he even mentioned the fee. At this point my long-suffering Jewish mother would discreetly explain that my father had spent the war years working in his uncle's café off Dalston Lane. Sometimes I wonder how much of my father has rubbed off.

'SHAKIN' ALL OVER'

In the summer of 1961 I got a job as a lifeguard at Brockwell Park, a fifteen-minute bike ride from the studio. Getting the job was a stroke of luck. Due to the hottest summer in a hundred years, the lido was packed and they needed all the lifeguards they could get, with or without a Life Saving Certificate. I didn't have a Life Saving Certificate. They gave me a test which I failed because I couldn't stay under water for longer than a minute without floating to the surface. But they were so short-staffed they gave me the job anyway and told me to pick up some tips for helping drowning people as I went along. I later discovered that only one of the other lifeguards was qualified and the tip you needed most for saving lives was a long pole with a hook on the end.

Life-saving paid well with plenty of overtime on account of the sunny weather bringing in the crowds. In the end I managed to save around a couple of hundred pounds and three small kids and one adult from drowning – one with the pole and two by making a spectacular dive into the shallow end before picking up the rescued soul in my arms and wading back to the steps. In my tea break I did some drawings which I later used to make a large painting called *Brockwell Park Lido*. All the people I knew at the lido are in it somewhere.

A lot of the young girls were nannies who worked for well-heeled Dulwich families. Anne was one. She had just turned sixteen and wanted to go to art school. We talked a lot about how she should get a portfolio together. Anne said she wanted to study at Camberwell, which she eventually did.

One afternoon she introduced me to her employers. Bill was a lawyer and collected art. His beautiful and warm-hearted wife was Margaret. In time Bill became my patron and bought over a dozen of my pictures, drawing and etchings. His daughter Louise now has them hanging in her Richmond home.

The other lifeguards were all good swimmers and three were professional wrestlers who wrestled in the evenings when they could get away early. One of them had been in the Merchant Navy and painted in oils the boats he had sailed in, which he showed me. They were pretty good for someone with no training. We got on well and he showed me lots of tips for self-defence because he'd learned his wrestling in Egypt where there were no rules and losers in a fight got badly beaten. In return I gave him a few hints on painting but he didn't really need any. He was a natural. I told him simple things like where to get cheap canvas and the name of the specialist shop on the Pavement, the street bordering Clapham Common where you could buy brushes wholesale. His name was Stan. He was short and stout and very strong.

Stan also played a few songs on the guitar and talked a lot about his ex-wife. He missed her. He said he blamed himself. After work we would spend time at my studio. He liked it there. His own modest flat was full of small oil paintings of places he had visited. He had kept postcards and used them as reference. A lot of his pictures were of Spanish and Egyptian ports. Malaga. Cadiz. Alexandria. Port Said. They were a bit like L.S. Lowry's paintings. Complex shapes reduced to the bones. And I must say that one port looked pretty much like another. Blue sky. White walls. Red roofs. Green sea. But maybe that is how it is with ports on the Med.

Stan said he wanted to be a professional painter like me one day, if things worked out and he could put enough by and the right place came up. And he didn't have to pay his ex-wife something each month. I viewed Stan as a jolly man but never really happy. I only saw him smile from the heart when he got a picture 'dead right'. It wasn't often. I have frequently wondered about Stan's need to paint pictures. A need that is in the soul of us all. You see it most clearly expressed in a child playing with crayons or pots of paint. That same calling continues as we age but only a few respond. The very great painters still work with a child's imagination. Van Gogh comes to mind. Rubens does not.

The big hit that summer was 'Shakin' All Over' by Johnny Kidd and the Pirates. The lifeguards would play it on the jukebox in the workman's café across from the pool where we spent our breaks. There had been plenty of rock and roll hits before 'Shakin' All Over'. Most were American. Records by Bill Haley, Gene Vincent, Jerry Lee Lewis, Little Richard, the Everly Brothers and Roy Orbison dominated the Top Ten. But the English attempts at rock and roll were, until Johnny came along, feeble by comparison. Tame as opposed to wild. No one would rip the seats out of cinemas – as they did when Bill Haley and his Comets sang 'Rock Around The Clock' – while listening to Tommy Steele singing 'Little White Bull'. Or the Shadows strumming 'Foot Tapper' in neat suits, doing a little dance routine and grinning. But 'Shakin' All Over' was the real thing. UK rock.

That summer, the hottest anyone could remember, was the turning point. In those long hot days Britain's youth ached for a new way to live. No more thinking of a dead-end life with a dead-end job in those dreary postwar days. No more

Teds. No more drab styles and rationing. Fags sold in packets of five and the pubs closed at ten. Maybe it was just a desire for something more exciting to sunbathe in. Or something stylish to wear walking in the sun. A place to go in the light hot evenings. A new shade of lipstick. A slim tie. Longer hair. Shorter skirts. A record that made you want to move.

If I was forced to pick a time when the Fifties officially came to an end and the Sixties began, it was the summer of 1961.

CHEEKY CHAPPIES

Sixty South Side is a large sprawling studio flat on the ground floor of a Victorian terrace, built in 1893, in Clapham. It has changed a little over the years since the time I moved in but not so much that you would notice. When the flat was mine the large walled garden had a fifty-year-old sycamore tree, rows of very tall untidy hollyhocks growing from an old rock garden, rose bushes, an unpruned privet, irises and daffodils in season, and dominating the north right-hand corner was a rusting but still usable air-raid shelter covered with moss.

The block overlooked Clapham Common and was right across the street from a pub. The pub was called the Windmill because there was once a windmill right on the spot where they built it. William Turner painted the part of the common from where the windmill stood around 1805 and you can see the painting in the V&A. It's more of a sketch than a painting. A lot of his pictures look like sketches, even though they took him months.

They served drinks to your table in the lounge of the Windmill pub on Sunday evenings until the mid-Sixties when Young's, the brewers who owned it, decided to become part of the 'Swinging Scene' and ripped out the traditional interior brass and wood furnishings, replacing them with bright paint and plastic. Before the Sixties makeover, a waiter in a white steward's jacket with gold buttons came round with a silver tray and took your order. At that time I would drink Guinness with Jimmy Wheeler until they called time. Jimmy was a six-foot overweight comedian with a tobacco-stained moustache and a large bloodshot nose. He had once been very big. As well as doing his own act, Jimmy wrote gags for Max Miller, who was known as 'The Cheeky Chappie'. Paul McCartney once told me that at the time Linda was about to go into the vegetarian frozen food business they were thinking of naming their veggie burgers 'Cheeky Chappies'. Clearly someone in marketing at Findus talked them out of it.

Jimmy lived in the cottage next to my studio. It had once been a coachhouse adjacent to the main house, a vast double-fronted Victorian mansion that had been converted into an up-market funeral director's called Ashtons. They later moved to a smaller building near Clapham North, having sold out to a property developer. Flats there now change hands for £2 million. Ashtons also buried my dad when he died in 1987. He died from a heart attack watching *This Is Your Life*. Sad though my mother was at her husband's passing, the irony did not escape her.

The cottage was one up and one down, and had a long thin garden that ran by the side of mine; it was never used apart from dumping empties. The bedroom was small and cramped. There was a king-size bed that I never saw made and a Thirties dressing table covered in bottles of perfume and Scotch. There was more Scotch in the kitchen where Jimmy and his wife spent most of their time. Jimmy's wife Betty had high cheekbones and big eyes and she always let her long dark hair hang loose. Betty chain-smoked while she knocked back the Scotch and laughed easily and seldom got out of her floral silk dressing gown until the afternoon. She once told me she had been an artist's model in Chelsea when she was my age, which was twenty-one then.

Drink killed Jimmy and then killed his beautiful wife. In some ways Jimmy reminded me of Peter Cook. Generous.

Funny in a highly original way. And they both drank themselves to death.

Jimmy did me a big favour by giving me the piano he bought for Winifred Atwell that she didn't want. Winnie Atwell was the first female black pianist to sell a million records. Her biggest hit was 'Black And White Rag', which she composed on what she called her 'other piano'. This was an old upright that she'd had all her life, and when she played 'Black And White Rag' on stage they wheeled the other piano on so she could play her big hit on it. Winnie made a hobby of collecting pianos. Her house was full of them. Winnie was also a fine classical pianist and recorded with the London Philharmonic. She was born on 27 February 1914 and died on 28 February (my birthday) in 1984.

I played that piano an hour a day until my fingers got strong and then I picked up tunes and started teaching myself how to read and write music. But it was hard going. It was only later when I became mates with film music writer Stanley Myers that I got to understand more about reading and writing music.

My studio was made up of two high and very large rooms. I painted and played music in the room with the shuttered windows that overlooked the Common and slept and ate in the room at the back. When the block of houses was built, the maids lived in the top flat and the basement was the kitchen. One afternoon sometime in 1964 I was in the studio working when a middle-aged man called by and said he had been born in the house. His name was Alan. He went on to tell me that his mother had had nine children there and he was the youngest. Alan's mother had taken the house over from her mother when she died in the Thirties.

At that time 60 South Side was just a single house. Not
flats. He showed me where the developers had made changes
to the central stairwell and how the rooms had been divided
and said my studio was the reception room which led to the
main passage. The glass-panelled door which was just behind
the front door was the original and had survived a bomb
that had fallen close by and broken more or less every other
window in the street. It was Alan who pointed out that the
date engraved on the window in the back room of my flat –
1893 – was the year the block was built.

Ralph Fothergill lived in the flat above my studio and it
had a balcony and French windows. Ralph was in his nineties
and had spent his life working in a double act on the stage,
walking on tightropes and juggling Indian clubs. He once
told me: 'I was tying up my shoelace backstage at the Victoria
Palace and the Duke of Windsor who had come to see the
show with Mrs Simpson leapfrogged over me and then said
could he do it again and I said yes and he did so. I had it put in
the programme that I once performed with the future king.' It
was the only story he ever told.

He practised his juggling in the garden and he was pretty
good for a man of his age. He only dropped a couple now and
then. Well, all the time actually, but no one was watching but
me. He also did tricks with a lasso but he'd lost his touch and
the rope did little more than twirl around his ankles. Ralph
had even less luck with the ladies who brought his meals on
wheels (he only ever ate the pudding, saying the meat was
too tough and the greens were slushy). He did his best to get
them sexually interested by showing them photos of himself
juggling at the Victoria Palace while taking his willie out. In
the end one lady reported him. He was warned only to receive

his dinner at the door and do nothing else. He died not long after. Old men live off their dreams. Not spotted dick or rice pudding.

The middle-aged man who lived over Ralph was a bachelor whose name was something like Mr Humble or Bumble, or possibly Rumble. He worked in the city and was very private. Kept himself to himself, as they say. He entertained unhappy-looking, pale-faced young men for tea during the weekend. He went out at seven in a bowler hat and came home at six. In spite of being a man not given to outward displays of cheeriness, he was always extremely polite, and if I was with a young lady, he would always tip his hat.

A young married and childless couple lived on the top floor where you could see right across The Vale to Highgate. It was a wonderful view, and like all the other flats in the block, it had undergone no modernisation apart from the installation of a proper loo and bath. All the features and fixtures were original; in Ralph's flat not even the wallpaper had been changed. Brian was a pilot who flew planes for BOAC and Sue was an air hostess. After a year or two, they changed airlines and went to live in Melbourne.

Their flat remained empty for a long time because no one wanted to climb up four steep flights of stairs. The landlord eventually asked me to help him find a tenant since he knew I knew a lot of people. First off, I found him Jim McCormack who was an alto player with a girlfriend who looked exactly like the French actress Marina Vlady with long flaxen hair and pale grey eyes. Jim had a serious drink problem and ran out of money quicker than he earned it. He died from drink not long after moving in. His girlfriend was called Jackie and pregnant when Jim died. She asked if she could stay with me at least until her baby was born. I would have been happy to have given Jackie a bed but my current girlfriend was not so keen. It was not through lack of sympathy but space. I did my best to help Jackie, but I kept our relationship, which developed into something very special, secret. I still feel a deep sense of regret that I was not able to do more. Jackie was a beautiful, gentle woman. She eventually found a flat in Richmond and a regular boyfriend to go with it. Which meant all was well.

The top flat remained empty for a while. The landlord cleared it of Jim's piles of manuscript paper and bottles, and then I found Eric Burdon for him. But Eric didn't stay long. He didn't stay anywhere long. I told the old landlord he would have to find his own tenants in future. I had other things to do.

MEETING PETER COOK

I first met Peter in the editorial office of *Private Eye*. He was standing alone in the middle of the room wearing a dark pin-stripe hand-tailored suit with a spotted tie and smoking a Rothmans cigarette. He had just returned from performing *Beyond the Fringe* in New York. It was early in 1963. Around noon. We were the only people in the building apart from the two girls who answered the phone and dealt with subscriptions, made afternoon tea and dished out the biscuits. In the early days of the *Eye*, girls were not employed to do anything else. They came from upper-class families so the tea was tasteless and the tiny biscuits came from Fortnum & Mason. No one but me noticed.

Peter was at that time the most beautiful man I had ever seen. His eyes were very much like those of a giraffe. They were very large and they dominated his long face with its wide clean-cut mouth and square chin. His eyelashes were so long they looked false and his skin was fresh and without blemish, and he kept his hair very neat and shaved close. It was the look that you see in people from the upper class but Peter never once gave me the faintest hint he was upper-class. Or any class. He was simply funny in a way no one else was funny.

Peter introduced himself. 'Peter Cook,' he said in a way that suggested I might not have known and shook my hand. In spite of his fame Peter was always deferential when meeting strangers. He never assumed that someone he had never met would automatically know who he was. His expression suggested he did not know me. I told him my name and that I had been working at the *Eye* for three months, having more or less replaced Willie Rushton who was busy on the telly. He took it in and said he was pleased to meet me.

Peter had just become the major shareholder. He was concerned, as we all were, about the sudden and sharp decline in sales and general slowing down of interest in the satire movement. At satire's peak in the first two years of the Sixties, the *Eye* had been selling 90,000 copies and the satirical television show *That Was The Week That Was* (*TW3*), fronted by David Frost, was watched by nine million. Peter's show, *Beyond the Fringe*, played to packed houses. But by 1963, satire for the masses was no longer a novelty. It was more a case of satire for the few. The *Eye's* circulation had shrunk to under 10,000 and *TW3* was no longer the big draw.

Later that day, there was an editorial meeting about what we could do to save the magazine from going under and it was concluded without an obvious solution. Peter was unusually quiet throughout the meeting. His big eyes seemed to be focused elsewhere. After the meeting was over he lit a cigarette and sat down at the office typewriter (which is something he never did again) and wrote the first chapter of a series that was to become so popular it saved the magazine from folding. The first paragraph read:

The exact number of the Brethren at any given time is always hard to calculate but it can be safely said that a figure of two would be exact. To say the BODILY SEIZING OF YOUNG WOMEN is at least part and parcel of our belief would be no exaggeration.

'Tales of the Seductive Brethren' was an instant hit. It was one of Cooke's most imaginative inventions. Sales doubled week on week and the *Eye* soon regained its earlier popularity. The strip was drawn by Nicholas Garland in the style of *Mad* magazine artist Will Elder and written by Barry Humphries. Garland went on to become the political cartoonist of the *Daily Telegraph* but I have always thought his McKenzie drawings to be his finest hour. The strip led to a full-blown movie and helped to make the then little-known Foster's Lager a major brand.

At the same time Peter was contributing to the *Eye*, he was also building his double act with Dudley Moore. As the Pete and Dud telly shows took off, Peter was less able to spend afternoons joining in the joke sessions. When he did turn up he would bring a briefcase to carry his dozens of packets of extra long Rothmans and a silver cask of Scotch wrapped in a paper bag. The briefcase also contained a copy of a sex magazine that had a centre spread of a naked blonde being spanked by a man who Peter imagined looked exactly like Edward Heath. Peter was determined that we publish it and thus expose Heath's secret love life. But no one else saw the likeness and the images of the spanked man with a wide grin and fat belly never got beyond Peter's briefcase.

Heath's love life has been the subject of much speculation since his death. A love of sailing with its strapping Jack Tars and church choirs full of boys might offer a clue. There are other stories that tell of late-night visits by male prostitutes to Downing Street although I have no way of confirming their validity. Unlike the Profumo affair, Heath's private life was never going to present any obvious threat to national security, no matter how unsavoury. So I more or less ignored it.

ONE-MAN SHOW

I had my first one-man show of paintings and drawings in the Woodstock Gallery in Woodstock Street, just off Bond Street. The paintings were a mixture of pop portraits and pop compositions but with a satirical edge. The gallery was run by my former art teacher from the time I was a pupil at Archbishop Temple's, which was a cross between a grammar school and a secondary school built on a park adjacent to Lambeth Palace. At one point in its history Charlie Chaplin had been a pupil there, although you would only know that if you had been a pupil because the school made a big thing of it. This period of his early life at Archbishop Temple's does not appear in any of Chaplin's biographies. This is not the case with another famous old boy – the detective who arrested Derek Bentley for killing a policeman in Croydon during a botched burglary attempt by Bentley and his younger accomplice Christopher Craig in 1952. He was called Frederick 'Fred' Fairfax and he chased the two boys onto a warehouse roof. As a result, the nineteen-year-old Bentley, who had the mental age of a ten-year-old, was executed for a crime he did not commit. It was Craig who pulled the trigger but since he was under age they hanged Bentley instead.

Lyall Watson was a fine painter, an excellent teacher and a deeply committed socialist. Tate Britain own a number of his late works. Lyall ran his gallery to show young artists he thought had talent – not, as is usually the way, to get rich on the back of a fickle and gullible art market. He took only a very small commission, just enough to pay the rent and rates and make sure there was enough to advertise the shows and print decent invites. He still taught art while running the Woodstock Gallery and used some of his income to help keep the gallery going. Luckily he married the Mayoress of Lambeth and she helped him to obtain commissions such as painting murals in local schools and libraries. Lyall painted with great skill and imagination – I would say a bit like Daumier, the same broad monochrome brush marks and dramatic highlights.

The artists Lyall showed, being mainly fit and young, also helped with the upkeep. They repainted and made good the walls after each show and did any other repairs. One sculptor was in charge of the leaking toilet. A painter from Leeds looked after the lights. One from the Slade did carpentry jobs. It was very much a community. If someone had a good show and made a profit they would put some of it into a pot for others and to make sure there was always enough for a simple catalogue and wine and cheese on the opening night. There is a scene in Tony Hancock's great movie *The Rebel* in which he arrives in a Paris bar where all the young painters are exchanging ideas. They are a cheery lot. A little drunk but full of goodwill. It was a bit like that at Lyall's gallery. Just a little bit.

My show opened on 2 January 1963. It was the coldest day in 147 years and there was snow banked six feet high along the pavement of every road you walked down. No one was around and by nine the handful of people – my parents and close friends – were on the verge of calling it a day. Just as we were getting our coats a man suddenly stumbled through the door wearing a military-style mac, a hat you see bookmakers sport and a rosy complexion. He looked like a man who was no stranger to an opening night and free drinks.

He introduced himself as John Royden and said he was the art critic of the *Daily Express* and that all the pubs were shut because of the snow and that he was dying for a drop. He helped himself to a large glass of red wine and downed it in one. Carrying a second glass of wine, he toured the show, stopping a while at the painting of Marlon Brando, who I had painted as characters from his movies: as Terry in *On the Waterfront*, as Rio in *One-Eyed Jacks*, as Lieutenant Christian Diesti in *The Young Lions*, and as Stanley in *A Streetcar Named Desire*. The *Daily Express* art critic, smelling strongly of booze and fags, said he liked it. We all held our breath. He moved on. Looking. Nodding. Not making notes. Drinking. Then he reached the near-life-size painting of the Duke of Edinburgh in his underwear.

I had painted him as a child's cut-out surrounded by a selection of his uniforms. Head Boy Scout. Head of the Navy. Head Polo Player. John Royden knew a story when he saw it – 'East End Jew Mocks Duke', 'Satire Strikes The Palace', 'Pop Painter Pokes Fun At The Royals'. Downing his third red, John thanked me for the invite and said he had to get back to the office, adding that he assumed he was the first critic to have seen the show. We assured him that he was not only the first but the only critic. This pleased him and he had another glass of wine before stumbling out the way he had stumbled in.

The following morning the phone rang early. It was Lyall. The *Daily Express* had run a review and the *Evening Standard* had picked up the story. I was to get to the gallery at once because there was a photographer waiting to take a picture of me and the painting. The picture appeared on the front page of the midday edition. It was a headline story. By the early evening, an American textile magnate from West Chester, Pennsylvania, rang and bought *The Duke in His Underpants*. Later that evening the gallery got a call from L.A. The man introduced himself as Chopsey Pelter. He announced that he was a big name on the west coast. He went on to say that he wanted to buy the whole show, lock, stock and barrel. But most of all he wanted to get hold of *The Duke in His Underpants*. He said it was a world-famous picture. Like van Gogh and all those boys. When we reluctantly told him the picture had been sold he was unfazed. 'Paint me one the same' was his instant response. 'No one will know as long as no one says nothing.'

Chopsey then said he would send over someone from his legal department to tie up the deal and hung up. We looked at each other. No one sells out their first one-man show. There had to be a catch. But what? Catch or not, I went home and got to work on version two of the *Duke in His Underpants*.

THE PLACE TO GO

Around 1966 a very small and very trendy restaurant opened on the King's Road. I cannot actually recall the name of the restaurant but I do recall the people who ate there. I have them in the address book I kept from that time. I file under first names. Page one opens with Annie Nightingale's phone number and Brighton address and the book ends with Zoot Money's. I never knew where Zoot lived. I saw less of him than Annie.

If my address book is anything to go by, the clientele included the following. Mr and Mrs Michael Caine, some of the Stones, a few Who's, scriptwriters Dick Clement and Ian La Frenais, Tom Courtenay when he wasn't filming on location, Sean Connery and his wife Diane Cilento, George Best and someone else's wife, Cubby Broccoli and his cigar, Ossie Clark with Celia Birtwell and/or Alice Pollock, P.J. Proby and his joint, Jean Shrimpton, David Bailey, Terrence Donovan, Anita Pallenberg, Andrew Loog Oldham, Rod Steiger and his wife Claire Bloom (who lived next door), David Lean, Brian Duffy, a Beatle or two when not on tour, David Hemmings, Twiggy (then only seventeen) and her much older squeeze Justin de Villeneuve, someone from the BBC Drama Department looking for talent and only let in because he happened to be a dear friend of the head waiter ... I think I saw Harold Pinter but I certainly saw Vivienne Merchant, Spike Milligan who, like me, was a vegetarian and didn't like the food, Peter Osgood, Dick Lester, Robert Fraser and a boyfriend, Robert Freeman, David Frost and a girlfriend hoping to get on in showbiz, Peter O'Toole, Rita Tushingham, Julie Christie, Dudley Moore, Tom Gilbey and I think Vidal Sassoon popped in for a bite from time to time.

This group of people (plus a few others) made up the core of Sixties London. I also ate there. Swinging London could be fitted into one small restaurant. It did not matter that the food was indifferent and expensive. It mattered that you were one of the chosen. You didn't go for the soufflé that tasted like a Yorkshire pudding or the undercooked sweet peas. You went to reaffirm your status as being the first elite of the Sixties revolution. If we had thought of it at the time, we probably would have had cards printed and badges. But our names were enough. They always are if they are the right ones.

The wrong names waited outside. A long line desperate to get in. Night after night hairdressers from Hendon and car dealers from Croydon queued in the hope of getting a seat and rubbing shoulders with John Entwhistle, or at least getting a glimpse of him in the poorly lit room. Now and again the owner would let a couple in. They would be seated at the table by the kitchen door, which was next to the toilets. The idea was to make the famous feel more so. You can only be famous when you are with someone who isn't. In a room full of celebrities how would you know?

THE DUKE'S PANTS AND GOOSE SHIT

By the end of the first week of my show at the Woodstock, *Life* magazine sent a photographer to take a picture of *The Duke of Edinburgh in His Underwear* (the original title) and ran it over the whole back page in the following edition. The same evening BBC TV's art show *Monitor* came to film. The presenter was Huw Wheldon. He was a deeply self-satisfied man who had nothing interesting to say about art or anything else and was therefore ideally suited to work at the BBC. He turned up in green wellingtons and a smug smile and wandered around looking at the pictures for a couple of minutes, then came over to me. 'Blake?' he snapped in a manner that was to tell me he knew Peter Blake's work and that mine was nothing more than a copy. I knew he meant Peter Blake but I replied innocently that I preferred his poetry to his paintings and prints. I suggested that William's religious and spiritual convictions had less appeal when drawn. Words offered images, images offered themselves, and so on. But he was gone. Green-wellied off to find another pair of ears.

Later that month Chopsey arrived. The Californian who had promised to buy my exhibition in toto plus the new version of *The Duke in His Underpants*. He was a small man with sharp eyes and expensive clothes that he somehow made look cheap. He smoked cigars and my guess is that back home he'd carry a gun and use it when he had to. B-Feature hood was written all over him. Chopsey met me at his hotel, and over a drink told me he had made his fortune selling expensive houses along the coast road that runs from Los Angeles to

San Francisco, in particular around Carmel. Chopsey said that his father had been a bootlegger during Prohibition and kept geese to disguise the fumes from his underground distillery. 'If the cops raided the place, all they got a smell of was the geese,' he told me proudly. 'You gotta believe it. Goose shit smells real bad.'

It transpired that it was on this same land, free of goose shit and corn liquor odours that Chopsey Pelter built the homes that produced his multi-million dollar empire – and a very small fraction of which would go towards him getting his hands on my paintings, mainly the D of E in his smalls.

In the end it was not a simple deal. The small print included reshowing the entire collection in L.A. with me getting only a very meagre percentage. But a show in the States? No one in their right mind would turn it down. Even if it went sour, the publicity alone would be worth it. I could see the details of my shows in the next catalogue. Bond Street and Los Angeles. We agreed.

The deal was brokered by a young man called Marvin Mitchelson. Marvin made a great deal of money as a Hollywood divorce attorney. He represented one partner of just about every screen star who bust up during the Seventies and Eighties, and would make a name for himself by introducing the concept of palimony. His clients read like the cast list of one of those big budget all-star movies so popular at the time. *The Longest Day* becomes *The Shortest Marriage*, starring Robert De Niro. Sylvester Stallone, Zsa Zsa Gabor, Mickey Rooney, Joan Collins, Bianca Jagger . . . The fees Marvin picked up for helping unhappy Hollywood couples put him in the same financial league. His mansion was as big as they built them and his collection of Rollers was second to none.

The exhibition was to be reshown at the Comora Gallery. The paintings were packed and sent to the USA and we paid for everything. Shipping. Packing. Customs. The lot. We got a short letter from Marvin to say they had arrived and then nothing. Total silence. When we tried to call Chopsey and Marvin we could never get through. It was as if the whole deal had never existed.

After a couple of years we got a letter saying we could have the pictures back if we paid for the shipping. But not *The Duke in His Underpants*. Chopsey was hanging on to that one. His bootlegging old man would have approved.

My paintings and monotypes were last seen on the walls of Marvin's ex-wife, the Italian actress Marcella Ferri, by an American film producer pal who was visiting her. (The mansion is now owned by Johnny Depp.) When I discovered this I wrote and asked for them back, since they were not hers. Ferri's reply was that they had been put in the garage for safekeeping while the mansion was being redecorated, but the garage had burned down along with my paintings. I did not believe her.

Subsequent attempts to get my paintings back have all failed. I even hired a private detective but nothing came of it. I have no idea where my work is now. Covered in goose shit I suspect. As for Marvin, he spent a lot of time in jail for tax fraud before he died of cancer in a rehabilitation centre in 2004.

7

IN MY STUDIO

During the Sixties not a day passed without a pal dropping in to my studio. It's just off the South Circular which made it a convenient stopping-off point for pals coming back from an out-of-town gig. Some of my pals were famous. Pete Townshend once dropped by to ask me if I knew anything about a vintage Cadillac for sale down the road in Balham. Paul McCartney would come over from his house in St John's Wood to talk about painting. Marianne Faithfull spent time with me working on songs. Ray Davies's visits often had no special purpose. We were just pals hanging out. But he did once drop in to play a song he had composed while driving home from a gig. He used my guitar to play it. The song was called 'Little Donkey', a gentle Christmas song. It was three in the morning. High summer. Ray crooning the lullaby sitting on a stool by an open window. A slight breeze rustling the leaves on the giant sycamore . . .

Bill Vallas was not famous. He was my postman, and he would stop off for a cup of tea after work. Bill was a war hero, although he never mentioned it and I only found out when his widow Rita asked me to help clear out Bill's things after he died. All he ever told me was that he served in Italy at the end of the war. What he didn't say was that his small unit of machine gunners had held off a strong German advance from the ridge of a mountain village near the French border for six days until American troops arrived from Lombardy. They had no food and little water. It was a small but important victory, one of many that helped to turn the tide of the war in the Allies' favour. Rita had kept Bill's wartime photo albums. There was one photo taken in the Italian village, or what was left of it. Rita also had a suit that the villagers had made for Bill that she kept with his old uniforms (military and Post Office) in the wardrobe. Bill told Rita that when the Americans moved on they left behind any equipment not needed for the next push. In this instance they left tents and parachutes. Enterprising local tailors, having no material as a result of the war, quickly helped themselves to the canvas tents and made them into suits. They used parachute silk for the lining. And there, amongst his belongings, was a photo of Bill in his canvas suit alongside Luigi who had made it.

A twelve-year-old lad called Paul Douglas who wanted to be a painter one day, and has become a highly respected mural artist, would call in on his way home from school. He'd wait outside the large windows until he saw me and then wave. It was his way of telling me he wanted a lesson. I let it be known that if I wasn't busy, 60 South Side was an open house. Day or night.

There was a piano and drum kit. No one complained if there was live music. And there was a comfortable spare bed and clean sheets for anyone in need of a little extra sleep. Or maybe found sudden romance and had nowhere else to go. Sometimes I was host to someone I had not even heard of. This was more the case once I had made a name for myself on television. Some were teenage girls wanting an autograph. Now and then I'd get visits from art students asking for tips on how to get on in the art world. One seventeen-year-old came all the way from Denmark to get my autograph and stayed a week.

I painted mostly at night, all through the night. I have always preferred working nights to days and I had special lights put in that imitated natural daylight because normal house lights distort colours. Jimmy Wheeler came in after the Windmill closed with a crate of beer and a bottle of whisky and we talked and drank while I painted until dawn. I liked having Jimmy around when I painted because he had met quite a few of the people I painted and he would tell me something about them. When I was painting Carmen Miranda he told me: 'I worked with Carmen Miranda when she came over here. She had all her family working for her in her band. Half of them couldn't tell one end of an instrument from the other. She told me she'd been on the game before she got into show business and I told her she wasn't the only one. And a lot went back into it when the bookings dried up.'

Later in the Sixties Roy Hudd came to live in Clapham, close by, so we would meet up now and then. Jimmy said that Max Miller was the richest man he knew but he never bought anyone a drink. He told me that if you saw Max in a pub he'd tell the barman the round was on him, but when it came to paying, he'd pop to the toilet. Max Miller was Roy's idol and he commissioned me to paint a life-size picture of Miller in his stage outfit made from fancy curtains, a white hat, white make-up and red and white football socks. I did the picture twice: once for Roy and once for myself because Max Miller made me laugh before *Private Eye* and satire and Peter Cook, and there wasn't much else apart from *The Goon Show*. Max Miller got fired from the BBC for telling what people called a blue joke but his funniest stories were more surreal than blue. I am sure that Max Miller in his later years was a founding father of Sixties satire. He was for me.

This is one Jimmy Wheeler wrote for him. Surreal. A René Magritte of gags. 'I was in a pub the other night and this geezer comes up to me, sells me a bunch of asparagus. So I go home and the missus is in bed and I put this bunch of asparagus on the kitchen table and in the morning she starts yelling up at me, "Max, Max," and I say, "What?" and she says, "Max." And I say, "What?" and she says, "That bundle of firewood you brought home last night." And I say, "What firewood?" So she says, "On the kitchen table. It's damp. It won't light.'"

Jimmy was for me the Peter Cook of his day. When his doctor told him to stop drinking because it was killing him, Jimmy told him to fuck off.

The portrait I did for myself ended up being reproduced along with a lot of my other portraits of people I admired in a series called 'Childhood Heroes' in the *Observer* colour section, which had just started up as a rival to *The Sunday Times*. The art director who bought the rights to reproduce the portraits was Romek Marber. Romek is considered one of the great designers. As well as designing the *Observer*'s colour section, he designed hundreds of top quality covers for Penguin Books. At the time of writing Romek is still active, aged ninety-two.

8

THE GIRL NEXT DOOR

You won't have heard of Angela Scully. She was seventeen when I met her. She looked after her house-bound father and six-month-old daughter in the top flat next door at 58 South Side. Angela had just been ditched by the baby's father and just about survived on what the state paid her and a handout from her dad. Mr Scully lived in a wheelchair. He spent his life joining book clubs and record clubs and subscribing to magazines to keep in touch with the outside world. His flat was filled with boxes of long-playing records he couldn't play because he didn't have a gramophone. Day after day, Mr Scully sat at the kitchen table cutting bits out of newspapers and magazines and sticking them into large scrapbooks that Angela got him from Woolworths on Clapham High Street. When he died there were over a hundred, dating back to just before the war, when he had lost the use of his legs.

Angela had a dancer's body, a long neck and small breasts. She was what people call petite when they don't want to call them short, just about making five feet without shoes. Her cheap stockings always had runs in them. But her eyes were lovely, a deep soft chestnut brown, and they more than made up for her broken front tooth and the long hair she could never get quite right. And she tried. The colour changed. Golden blonde. Ash blonde. Jet black. Red highlights. It got cut short. Pulled back in a ponytail. She once tried plaits. When I last saw her, some thirty-odd years later, following a spell in the USA, it was a bright pink and green Mohican.

Between tending to her father's needs and those of her

daughter, Angela came to see me. She usually dropped by every day, even if it was only to say she was going to the shops and did I want anything. I grew to love Angela. She had great courage and an open honesty that might have led her to sainthood in another age. Nothing was too tough for her. Her miserable old man and her demanding daughter were just part of her daily life and she never once complained. We became lovers in the precious few moments of her free time.

My bed was in the corner of a large all-purpose room that had wooden window shutters you could fasten with a flat iron bar, and I would shut out the light by closing the shutters and Angela and I would make love. Often in complete silence. Afterwards I would lie back and dream a little with my eyes open and when I turned my head I could just see the top of the sycamore tree in the gap between the top of the shutters and an illegible name carved into the window frame, with the date 1893. Angela's large dark eyes were always closed. She dreamed only of a future free to do as she pleased. I dreamed only of fame.

When her father died, Angela took me to her flat. It was like a junkyard and she told me to help myself to all the records and anything else I wanted. I took a lot of the scrapbooks because her father had an eye for an interesting picture or story and I used some pictures for reference in my illustrations. Then there were the records. These were boxed sets that they sold at the time through magazines and newspapers. You subscribed and they sent a box every month. Mr Scully's were mainly Deutsche Grammophon recordings. Quality mostly. David Oistrakh. The Amadeus Quartet. Wilhelm Kempff. He had also invested in a complete edition of *Encyclopedia Britannica* that took up a whole shelf. I thought about it, but Angela and her dad lived on the top floor. Four flights. All those books. Up and down. I just took the records.

Angela went to America after she buried her father and we wrote to each other regularly. She wrote letters which were often twenty pages long and sometimes used a whole writing pad. She wrote with a clear childlike hand all the details of how she had married an ex-soldier who said he was a farmer but lived in a caravan on the edge of a small town in Virginia and how he beat her. Angela had another daughter. The beatings got worse. She got divorced but lost custody of the baby. With nowhere to live, Angela headed for New York.

The only job she could find, since she had no skills apart from caring, was in a hospice looking after dying junkies. But dying junkies are bad news. When she had been beaten up and raped once too often she decided to go and live in Ireland. Her father had been born there and came from a large family who lived in a small village. She worked her passage to Dublin and then hitched a lift to a village near Durrow in County Kilkenny, where Angela found lots of Scullys who remembered her father and were happy to take her in.

Angela then became the common-law wife of a farmer. Her letters grew less frequent and shorter but they were always full of hope. Her life would now be better. There would be a chance to grow. The past was behind her as far as she was concerned and the luck of the Irish was on her side. From time to time she enclosed a photo. Apart from the continuing search for the ideal hairstyle and need of cosmetic dentistry, Angela seemed hardly to have changed.

The last picture Angela sent me, following an unusually long gap, showed her with pink punk hair, an earring in her nose and a fixed front tooth. In the letter that came with the

photo Angela wrote that she had always dreamed one day
we might live together, although she knew in her heart that
this could never happen. She ended with the same deeply
touching reminder that, of all the men she had known, I was
the one she truly loved. The last page of her last letter was full
of giant childish kisses. I still have the letter. And the photo.
And the memory of her love.

9

PAUL'S HARMONIUM

While mooching around the studio Paul McCartney often played my harmonium. One day he asked if I knew anyone who sold them. I told him that my old Camberwell art school mate Paddy Lovely helped pay the rent by selling small organs and harmoniums. He picked them up from churches which were being knocked down for offices or being gutted and turned into community centres. Paddy also sold pews. Prayer chairs. Italian marble fonts. Carved mahogany lecterns. Oak altars. He even had a set of five early nineteenth-century iron bells made by the Whitechapel Bell Foundry in his garage. They're probably still there.

Aged fourteen, Paddy Lovely painted like Goya. Everyone at Camberwell said so. But those born with genius are by nature seldom normal. Conventional. Run-of-the-mill. Paddy was unpredictable. Not easy to handle. He told crazy stories and told them in a way that made them entirely believable. And some were true, no matter how unbelievable. He would do things no one in their right mind would dream of. Dealers can not promote someone who arrives at a posh fancy-dress party naked except for a pair of black socks, as he did once, and tells the hostess, 'I've come as a Blackfoot Indian.' Not then you couldn't, not even with all the swinging goings-on.

Had he been easygoing and met the right people, it would be Paddy Lovely's name that would carry the accolade of 'Britain's Greatest Living Artist' and David Hockney would be struggling to get a job designing Christmas cards.

Paul and I drove to Paddy's place which was just off Brixton Hill behind the RACS baker's. As luck had it, Paddy had half a dozen in various states of repair and while his wife Belle made tea we looked the instruments over for one that had bellows without holes and a keyboard with all the keys. Paul chose a very nice single manual with a rosewood case and bellows with brass edging. Paul watched from a distance as Paddy and I carted the heavy instrument down five flights of stairs and stuffed it into the boot of my car. Paul paid Paddy thirty quid and I gave Paul and his harmonium a lift to St John's Wood.

There was something I noticed when Paul was a passenger. Normally he was conversational and had plenty of witty observations. But when sitting in a car he just sat staring in silence at the road ahead. His eyes seemed to say, 'Please, God, don't let anyone drive into us.' To be fair, I found a large left-hand-drive American car tricky to handle at times. Dents and scrapes everywhere. Or 'Don't make Barry forget what he's doing and drive into someone.' When we crossed Chelsea Bridge we faced a stream of busy oncoming traffic that made matters a lot worse. It was rush hour. I tried to take his mind off his projections of a premature death by telling him about Paddy's paintings and how he painted like Goya when he was fourteen. Paul did his best to pay attention but the endless line of speeding buses and lorries were foremost in his mind and my descriptions of Paddy's early masterpieces went over his head.

An hour later, having driven painfully slowly and at one point being overtaken by a dust cart doing 5mph, I parked in Paul's circular driveway. I heaved the harmonium out of the boot and dragged it into the hall. Paul got a chair and sat down and got the hang of filling the bellows with his feet at the same time as running his fingers over the keys. 'It's got a great sound,' he said and played a few chords. 'There's something very nostalgic about it.' I could see he was fascinated. I told him I would leave him to it and drove home.

The following morning Paul called and asked me to come over when I was free. I told him I'd come around lunchtime. Paul let me in with a smile and a handshake. 'I've been playing most of the night,' he said. 'I'll play you the song I've just finished.' The harmonium was exactly where we had put it the previous afternoon. In the hall, at the foot of the main staircase. He sat down and played and sang 'Your Mother Should Know'. He looked pleased and I told him I thought the harmonium really suited the song. He then ran through 'We Can Work It Out', using John's original harmonium backing.

From what I have read since, the relationship between Jane Asher and Paul had been on the edge for a full year before she announced to the press it was over. Others may have known how bad things were but it was not obvious to me at the time. I only saw them together now and then as she worked in movies and was not often at home when I was with Paul. And during the times we did spend together she seemed happy enough. But there is no way of telling what people do in private and I had no idea Paul was messing about with other women as seems to have been the case.

Thinking back to Paul sitting at the harmonium singing about life being very short and no time for fussing and fighting, there was perhaps a lot more personal history in both the lyric and the tone of voice than a brief impromptu performance demanded. I can only hear this song now in the context of the break-up of Paul and the future celebrity cake-maker and wife of *Private Eye* cartoonist Gerald Scarfe.

10

BRIGHTON ROCK

Although I knew of Annie Nightingale because she wrote a lot about pop music and appeared on the telly, I had never met her until she was a guest on *A Whole Scene Going*. She was a good talker and very beautiful, and at the time she was known as Anne. It is the name I called her then and still do. She arrived at the BBC studio in White City in a mustard mini skirt, suspenders and nylon stockings. When she sat down and crossed her lovely long legs her pretty pink knickers didn't have a lot of places to hide. It didn't bother her. Nothing much bothered Anne, and from what I read about her now, it still doesn't.

I shared interviewing guests on *AWSG* with Wendy Varnals, and Wendy did most of the interview with Anne. It was not until after the show that I got to talk to her. She said that she lived in Brighton and was married to a writer called Gordon Thomas and had a child. I told her that I had heard of her husband and knew his work. We talked more. Drank more. I smoked some pot. Maybe Anne did. It turned midnight. No trains. I asked her how she would get home. She said she hadn't thought about it. I remember saying I lived in Clapham and the BBC always provided a taxi.

Shortly after we became close friends, Anne suggested that I come to Brighton. I could meet Gordon and we would all have dinner together. I accepted the offer and I dined with them both many times in the years to come. Gordon was very much like Anne in that he said what he thought and had no time for crawlers. For example, when I mentioned I was pleased to have a show on the BBC, he said, 'The place is full of weak, small-minded men guarding their jobs.' In this instance, Anne held an opposing view, which was just as well as they were about to give her the job of first female disc jockey, one she is still doing. Gordon had made a lot of money from his writing and enjoyed nothing more than spending it, mainly on drink and in the local Indian restaurant.

Most nights the people dining in the Star of India were locals. The atmosphere was friendly, and apart from the occasional bloke who'd had a few too many lagers, there was never any trouble. But there was one night, following a Brighton race meeting, when it got out of hand. There were about six racegoers from out of town. Three couples in their forties. South Londoners by their accent. New rich. Gold watches and fake tans. They were pissed when they arrived and got more pissed as they tucked into their vindaloo. The men shouted instead of speaking, the women screamed when they laughed, and all of them were rude to the waiters. The noise became unbearable. Eventually Gordon said that he had had enough. He grabbed hold of Anne's bag, took out a handful of tampons, used a candle flame to light the tails as if they were sticks of dynamite, and jumped onto the table. 'Your evening's over!' he yelled and threw the smoking tampons into the air. Silence. Absolute silence. Apart from a pan of chicken tikka sizzling in the kitchen.

Anne later opened a boutique in Brighton as well as doing work on the radio. Gordon went to live in Ireland and Anne had another baby. Then she met someone she was happy to live with and told me it might not be as easy as it had been to see each other. And it was the case. We have not met since then and have spoken only once on the phone. I asked her to help with a campaign I was involved with to end noise pollution. Anne said that people should be allowed to make as much noise as they liked. Same old Anne. The campaign was a huge success and a Noise Pollution Act was introduced, and now you can't make as much noise as you want to without being fined or sent to prison. The leader of the campaign, Val Gibson, a tigerish and attractive blonde was given an MBE for her efforts.

Anne has become very secretive about her private life. If you look on the web you will find almost nothing about her two children, Lucy and Alex, or her hilarious life with Gordon or the man who replaced him (someone called Binky Baker). A lot of showbiz celebs are cagey about their history. Love children. Skeletons in the closet. All that sort of thing. Fair enough. Anne once told an interviewer that if people wanted to know about the men in her life they should ask them.

Gordon died in 2017, having married again and produced another family. His books continue to sell in millions. Anne carries on spinning the hits dressed as she did when I first met her. Mini skirts. The lot. No stopping Annie.

11

CHILDHOOD HEROES AND VILLAINS

The series of my paintings that appeared in the *Observer* colour section called 'Childhood Heroes' was originally painted for an exhibition at the Robert Fraser Gallery. Robert had seen my work and said he would give me a one-man show. This would have been around 1965 but he had no wall space free at the time and it would take place in a year or so. For a short while in the Sixties Robert Fraser's gallery in Duke Street was one of no more than a handful that would guarantee big sales and an international reputation. A lot of his clients were millionaire pop singers and movie stars, and Robert always made a big thing out of who he was selling to. In his hip designer suits, snappy hats and cool circular spectacles Robert Fraser was the 'in' dealer.

There were a couple of other art dealers who had seen that Pop Art was making money and decided to jump in while the going was good. One was called John Kasmin, who was known to his close circle of pals as 'Kas'. A graduate of Magdalen College, Kasmin had an eye for publicity and was initially responsible for forcing David Hockney onto the public and eventually becoming the 'Greatest Living British Painter'. Kasmin married Ben Nicholson's niece, which was not a disadvantage in making a name for himself in the art market. Another gallery that was up to date with changing styles belonged to Leslie Waddington. Les had a small group of big-name artists who he promoted with much energy and no lack of expertise. But Waddington was very precious and only showed his very small tightly-knit group of friends, who also happened to paint.

I got the invitation to show with Robert Fraser because I was considered 'in' at the time. But the show was cancelled. Old Etonian Robert, 'Groovy Bob' to his close circle of pals, had been at the now infamous drugs bust when the stoned Marianne and Mick were supposed to have been found on a sofa fooling around sexually with a Mars bar. They weren't. The press made it up. But the fuzz carted Groovy Bob off to the nick and charged him with possession of heroin.

There was an added bonus to Fraser not showing my work. As well as selling nearly all the work from my studio, the offer by the fledgling *Observer* colour magazine to reproduce the pictures in a six-week series meant they would be seen by millions, not just the select few at the private view and a trickle in the weeks that followed. It led me to form my Sixties view that art should be made available to as many people as possible. Popular. A magazine does this. A gallery wall, even one at the Tate Modern, does not. It is a view I still hold. Elitist art exists in a world that was never mine. I do not have a problem with a Picasso printed on a T-shirt. I have a problem with pricing a David Hockney art school composition at £92 million and making the art market worse than a bank robbery.

In the end it didn't matter about the show. I sold all the paintings of my heroes except Carmen Miranda. It was the first in the series and in my opinion the best. I haven't sold it because I haven't met anyone I like enough to sell it to but I did give Decca permission to use it as an album cover for Carmen Miranda's greatest hits. At a price. Another in the series was Baden-Powell. I liked his pale khaki-coloured uniform with yellow-edged scarf held by the leather toggle with the scout crest. I also painted William Brown of Richmal Crompton's

Just William books and a portrait of Beau Geste, which I sold to the *Observer's* advertising manager. He was a very nice American who went back to the States and sadly died of cancer soon after. Dick Clement (the writer of *Porridge*, director of *Ottley* and so many others) bought my portrait of Biggles for his wife's birthday. She sold it when they got divorced. The painting is now owned by the frontman of a rock band called The Bevis Frond who used it for an album cover.

After the Stones drug bust Fraser was put on trial and found guilty. He spent six months in jail but did not recover from his addiction or reckless lifestyle. On his release he continued to use drugs and have unsafe sex with men. He died HIV-positive in 1986. Although he was supposed to be an art expert, nothing Fraser ever said convinced me. Sex and drugs were his thing. That and being groovy.

12

HOW THE JOKES ARE MADE

Joke sessions at the *Eye* haven't changed in fifty years. The new editorial team led by Ian Hislop follow the same pattern as that created by Richard Ingrams, Christopher Booker and myself. For a long period Cook sat in when he was free. John Wells worked with Richard but never with Christopher or me. John and Richard wrote 'Mrs Wilson's Dairy', which was extremely funny and popular with the readers. Mrs Wilson was renamed Gladys and she wrote poetry, as did the real Mrs Wilson. The diary portrayed life at Number Ten as a cosy northern home rich with lower-middle-class aspirations. Wilson himself was always referred to as Wislon in the *Eye*, and the diary was eventually turned into a musical directed by Joan Littlewood. It became a West End hit, and so did 'Dear Bill' two decades later, which John and Richard also wrote. John starred as Bill when not spending romantic evenings at the home of Princess Margaret.

Ian Hislop (Hizza to his *Eye* intimates) joined as a contributor in 1986. I retired when I reached seventy. I do not know the names of the writing team today, apart from Nick Newman, who was a contributor at the time I was part of the editorial joke team. I know only that the *Eye* has never been more popular or sold more copies. Make of that what you will. There are other teams at the *Eye* who write gossip, which was very much an Ingrams' thing, plus in-depth stories about corrupt local councils, which was very much Paul Foot's thing. I played no part in either but I did invent 'Colemanballs'. I still keep in touch with Ian and he tells me nothing has really changed. The form and style follow that laid down by the original writers. E.J. Thribb continues to appear. As does Silvie Krin.

Writing the joke pages takes place two afternoons a week and the morning of Press Day. One of the biggest changes in producing the *Eye* is the moving of Press Day from Sunday to Monday. This is because Monday's papers are more newsworthy than Sunday's. Sunday papers do little more than rehash the previous week's news, along with publishing unreadable sections on gardening, which car to buy and where to go on your holiday. By contrast, Monday's news is fresh. The main reason for this is that the majority of weekday journalists take Saturday off and start their working week on Sunday. The Monday editions of national newspapers carry the latest stories, and the latest stories are obviously vital when it comes to making topical jokes.

Press Day is still the most important day of the fortnight. It involves doing the cover, which time has shown heavily influences sales. A feeble joke on the cover will wipe out a large chunk of street sales. A great cover will add thousands. In the early years Press Day began with lunch at Jimmy's, a cheap and gloomy Greek basement restaurant in Frith Street. The eponymous owner Jimmy was overweight and balding. He wore a dirty apron and never once smiled. His food was basic and had not much to do with Greece. There were some stale olives but not a lot else, although his chips were pretty good and would have been even better had he served them hot. We went there because no one else did and we could have the place to ourselves. At a table in the corner we would think up the cover joke and captions for news stories. Apart from the lunch at Jimmy's, all the other jokes are written in the editorial office.

The way jokes are written for *Private Eye* is, as far as I know, unique. I believe there is nothing like it anywhere, except perhaps in script sessions at an American TV company. I once read that an episode of *Cheers* involved up to twenty writers pitching in gags like dealers on Wall Street. But that is telly and not the printed page. The *Eye* contributors sit around a cheap desk on three Victorian chairs which came with the office. When a joke session takes place the editor writes down the jokes with a biro on pink bank paper that then gets taken to the room with a typewriter and typed up and stuck down on another sheet of larger paper and then sent off to be printed. The jokes are thrown in verbally by everyone present and the joke that gets the biggest laugh gets in. Sometimes a good joke is made better by someone else's take on it. And then made even better by another. But the man with the biro and pink paper (Ingrams then, Hislop now) has the last say, and once a joke is written down, it is seldom, if ever, changed.

Bad taste jokes were often a cause of disagreement but it only rarely reached boiling point. It was during the height of the Troubles that Ingrams decided to put Bernadette Devlin on the cover. She was in a mini skirt, being shouldered by loyal supporters, and the crotch of her knickers was clearly visible. The caption Ingrams came up with was 'This should get a rise out of Paisley'. Foot took against it. He thought it cheap and in bad taste. Foot was a Devlin supporter and threatened to resign if the cover was printed. Ingrams, who was always a Catholic sympathiser and has since converted, went ahead and printed the cover, in spite of possibly losing the best journalist in Britain. The joke caused much amusement everywhere – apart from the Falls Road.

Foot did not resign and continued to work at the *Eye* until he died suddenly from heart-related problems in 2004. I suspect the fact that he and Ingrams had been pals since they met at Shrewsbury had a lot to do with the reason Paul did not carry out his threat. Old boys. Loyalty. A school tie is thicker than water. And pragmatic, where else would Paul have had the freedom to attack corruption as openly as he did?

The *Eye* now uses breaking news on the telly to keep up to date with stories on Press Day. Even if it had been available in the Sixties, Ingrams would not have used it. He did not learn to drive until he was forty and he still can't type.

13

MY FRIEND ACROSS THE RIVER

When you take the Northern Line from Clapham Common to Soho or to the theatres on Shaftesbury Avenue or to the offices of *Private Eye*, the station to get off at is Leicester Square. It is central to all these places and also leads to Chinatown. In the Sixties it had no more than a handful of restaurants with steamy windows full of flattened-out ducks coated in glossy dark brown fat hanging upside down. And inside you could see chefs chopping them into slices and serving soup that smelled like dirty laundry water with garlic. Only the Chinese ate there. There were no tourists. Today Chinatown takes up the entire area of South Soho. It is a microcosm of London itself – a tourist attraction lacking both a heart or history. Then South Soho consisted of just two streets.

Gerrard Street was one. It ran the whole length of South Soho and was full of Chinese mini-supermarkets and Chinese tea rooms. You could buy rice out of sacks and vegetables imported directly from Hong Kong in the supermarkets and buns covered in pink icing in the poky little tea rooms. I sometimes did both. The other was Lisle Street. At the Piccadilly end was a basement club called the Kaleidoscope which was used as a rehearsal room during the day. In 1964 I would buy the *Melody Maker* each Friday and check through the Musicians Wanted ads.

Although I was making some decent money from my work at the *Eye* and other magazines, plus the week in every month I taught painting and life drawing at Croydon Art School, I always found I was a little short. Painting materials were expensive and still are in the UK. I had passed my driving test and bought a period white American saloon that needed a lot of money to keep it running. The gearbox was worn, and being American was expensive when it came to getting parts. I made the extra playing jazz. One weekend in March 1964, I saw an ad for a tenor player in the *Melody Maker*. The ad said the band was new. Being formed. I made a call and learned that the audition was for the coming Saturday in the basement of the Kaleidoscope. The voice on the phone said that we would start at three. I said I would be there.

It was raining heavily. It had been raining all week. I took the Northern Line to Chinatown and made my way to the club. I pressed the bell and waited in the rain. Nothing. Then I hammered for a while on the glass door and eventually a black guy with a friendly face opened the door. 'Thanks for coming,' he said, inviting me in. 'I hope you haven't been waiting too long but the bell doesn't work and I've been setting up the sound system and I can't hear a thing with the phones on.' I told him not to worry.

He said his name was Hamilton King and he was the bandleader. As I was soon to discover, he was also the band's drummer. Hamilton led me into the main room that was already set up for rehearsals and introduced me to the other musicians who were auditioning. They were Ray Davies and his brother Dave. Pete Bardens was sitting at the piano. We waved to each other. Pete Quaife had a bass guitar round his neck and offered me a cigarette.

After discussing what songs we might rehearse, it quickly became evident that as musicians we had no common ground. Hamilton was rock and roll. Ray, Pete and Dave leaned towards rhythm and blues. Pete Bardens had a touch of boogie-woogie about his style and I was at a point in my life when I worshipped John Coltrane. We talked it over for about an hour and even then we couldn't find a tune we all knew.

The problem was that there was no repertoire for rock and roll as there is now. Today you can go into a music shop or click on Amazon and find hundreds of books full of the 'Greatest Rock Hits Ever'. But not in the early Sixties. You picked up what you could from records and, as a result, bands played any old thing from Chuck Berry to Perry Como.

After thinking hard for a while Ray said why don't we try 'Money' and we ran it through. I was standing next to Dave at the mic across from Ray. He had this gap between his front teeth and sang with the same voice he talked with. Everything about Ray, his manner, his presence, his style and not least his musicianship indicated he was going to make a lot of money. I only got to know about his genius for writing later.

When the three-hour rehearsal was over Hamilton thanked us all for coming and handed out our expenses, which included something for a bite to eat as well as travel. You seldom even got your train fare and I considered this a promising gesture. If we ever got a band together the signs were that we might also get paid. Mostly you came away from a gig out of pocket unless someone gave you a lift there and back and someone else bought you a drink.

As things worked out none of us were hired and I am fairly certain Hamilton never made it to the big time. Or even small time. I did keep my eyes open in case his name showed up somewhere, but he vanished as far as I could tell. But the day was historic. For me at any rate. I met Ray, who was to become a lifelong pal. After we packed up our instruments we exchanged phone numbers and agreed to fix up a time to get to know each other better. But after all these years I am not sure if I do know him any better than on that first meeting. Not *really* know.

When a person is very deep, you never know the whole of it. Maybe you see more than they want to show but there is always something hidden. Even now, I know there are parts of him which possibly he himself never visits. At least, not for long. And I suspect there are times he feels the same about me. But in the end none of this matters. Genuine love of someone is beyond knowing them. Usually it is about what you don't know that keeps a relationship intact. The finding of more and more.

14

THE BIG HOAX

I had been working at the *Eye* for a couple of months when Richard Ingrams decided in the interests of the magazine and his personal career to sack Christopher Booker and take over the job of editing the magazine. Christopher was on his honeymoon at the time and in no position to offer any opposition. He had just married Emma Tennant, who was later to carve out a name for herself as a postmodernist writer. She died in 2017.

To get rid of Christopher, Richard asked everyone who was working at the *Eye* at the time to sign a round robin in which he claimed that Booker wasn't fit to edit the magazine as he was never there (partly true) and was unreliable (ditto), and what the magazine needed was a firm hand, not one given to signs of temper (true). Christopher once threw a typewriter out of a window, nearly killing a passerby (also true). Everyone signed, including me.

When Christopher got back from his honeymoon, he was effectively out of a job, while Richard had engineered a comfortable nine to five for himself. He would take a taxi from 22 Greek Street and catch the 5.30 from Paddington to his home in Goring-on-Thames in time for a spot of gardening before dinner. No one could blame him. He had a wife and a child and there would be more children in time. Richard was and is a family man. He also gave me a generous fortnightly salary of £15 a week for doing just about all the in-house artwork as well as cartooning and writing gags. When there was nothing else for me to do on the editorial side I helped Tony Rushton – Tone, as he is known to all – who at that time doubled selling ad space with laying out the magazine.

I knew a lot of people in Soho who had clubs and restaurants such as Ronnie Scott. Ronnie was a friend although he was fourteen years older. We had known each other a long time since our families came from the same part of Stepney – we lived just streets away from each other. Ronnie's family name was Schatt, and his father Jack played alto. So did Ronnie at first but he later switched to tenor. Ronnie advertised his then brand new club first in *Private Eye*.

Not long after I started working at the *Eye* I painted a mural in the editorial office, covering the entire wall with Pop Art images. I invited other cartoonists to contribute and we worked out a plan so we didn't turn up on the same day or paint the same faces. Willie Rushton had a genius for caricature which he did without reference. Gerald Scarfe and Ralph Steadman also contributed a few heads here and there. I didn't do caricatures for the mural: instead I opted to paint more formal portraits in the manner I had been taught at Camberwell Art School, and Ingrams, who is a gifted self-taught artist, did a brilliant portrait of Tone which got my vote as the best portrait on the wall.

After the mural was finished, we all agreed it would be a good idea to do other works. Over lunch at a pub on Cambridge Circus – we had not started to use the Coach and Horses regularly in the early days – Willie and I cooked up the idea of painting a picture together to hoax the Royal Academy's Summer Exhibition. Willie would draw faces of three Establishment stereotypes – a Catholic cardinal, a judge and an army general – which I would then transform into formal portraits. We decided to submit the painting under the name of Stuart Harris, which Ingrams thought up. Someone used the pub phone to call the Academy and find out when pictures had to be submitted. Sending in Day was less than three days away.

Willie drew the faces in five minutes, there and then, and handed them over. But the painting, canvas preparation and drying time . . . I knew that I would have to work day and night to get the painting ready in time.

I went home straight away and on the way decided to paint a work to the maximum proportions permitted, which were six feet by five. I didn't have a canvas that big so I nailed two pieces of hardboard together. I painted the three figures Willie had drawn sitting at a table covered with pop paraphernalia including Camp coffee, a half-eaten boiled egg and a box of Terry's All Gold chocolates (things that littered my studio). The cardinal had a copy of *Private Eye* and the judge was reading a sex mag with a naked woman on the cover so I called the painting *Nude Reclining*. The day before the picture was to be transported to the doors of the RA submissions department, the entire *Eye* staff, including the girls who made the tea, all came to 60 South Side and cheered me on to get it finished. It was a bit like the final stages of Roger Bannister running the four-minute mile.

At one in the morning I was done. I put a lot of drying agent in the oil paint and used fast-drying emulsion for the black background, which I left until last. I then put a simple flat wood frame round the picture and went to bed. Possibly a tea girl stayed the night to make sure I got up in time and had some breakfast before the Big Day.

Nude Reclining became the hit of the show. 'The RA Goes Pop' screamed one headline. 'Pop Goes the Summer Show!' screamed another. The *Sunday Times* art critic John Russell singled it out as a masterpiece of the Pop genre and everyone wanted to talk to Stuart Harris. Because he didn't exist the press grew desperate. They even phoned up the *Eye* to ask if we knew who he was. We said it was David Frost and that he had a hidden talent as opposed to no talent. 'Frost Hoaxes the RA' screamed more headlines.

Throughout the summer the press embarked on a frenzied attempt to locate the non-existent Stuart Harris and every time they called the *Eye* for a lead we would sell them a dummy. On the last day of the show Willie, Richard and I had lunch at the Seven Dials and decided the hoax would somehow be richer if the truth were known. We could say that the Royal Academy had been fooled and Stuart Harris, who had won the praise of so many, was none other than B. Fantoni and W. Rushton. I phoned a pal on the *Daily Mail* called Michael Bateman and gave him the scoop. The *Mail* printed a full-page account with a picture of me and Willie and the mild-mannered, balding, portly bespectacled secretary of the RA, Humphrey Brooke (looking bewildered), standing in front of the painting.

From then on I continued to use the name Stuart Harris for the majority of drawings I did for the *Eye*. I also used the name Gavin Prick, which Willie had invented for a trendy *Eye* fashion columnist. Willie was very funny. Always had been. Ingrams told me that when he was at prep school with Willie dissecting a toad in a biology class, the master held up a section of the toad's innards and asked Willie, 'What's this, boy?' Willie's reply was, 'Disgusting.'

Nude Reclining was sold to an architect called Richard Sheppard for £500. He hung the painting in the hall of his office. He was knighted in 1981 for his work in architecture.

15

PRICING ART

Selling paintings to friends is never easy and in the main I always prefer to offer a picture as a loan. That is to say a friend may keep it for as long as they want but should they grow tired of it I would have the picture back. One lifelong friend had six pictures hanging in his Norfolk home for over fifty years. All of them were painted in the early Sixties and include several from my childhood. There have been instances when a friend has insisted on paying me, as did Peter Cook. When I did an illustration of Pete and Dud for the *Radio Times* at the start of their new series Peter bought it. I painted Peter as Sherlock Holmes looking through a magnifying glass for a tiny Dud. I took it to the office and Peter paid me £175 in cash. Later that afternoon he asked for the money back because he had just lost a packet on a horse at Kempton Park. About a year later he gave me a cheque, with interest. As I was to discover after he died, it was the only painting Peter ever bought.

Commissions are different, like the picture of Max Miller I did for Roy Hudd. A commission makes the whole issue of value a lot easier. The decision has been agreed by both parties in advance. It is how I fixed prices as an illustrator and the system worked perfectly. When a client calls and asks for artwork there will be a deadline and a budget. Three days' work, say, at my daily rate and extra if the job involves travelling or a lot of research. Once I was hired by *The Sunday Times* to do drawings of the Pakistani cricket team on tour. This meant hotels and so on. Another commission was to cover a race meeting at Brands Hatch. My fee would always include expenses. Several jobs I did for the *Observer* colour magazine meant days of research at the Imperial War Museum. Again, the fee reflected that time spent in research.

The problem with pricing fine art is that art has no commercial value other than what people are prepared to pay for it. And it can't be about the time taken on a picture. The man hours. Painting pictures is not like house painting or plumbing. An artist's time is cumulative. It is about experience gained over a long period, in many cases from early childhood. Aged seventy, you might be looking at sixty years and more of learning. Each new canvas carries with it all that you have learned from those painted previously. Hundreds and hundreds. I think this is why many painters prefer to have a dealer look after that side of things. I usually ask the buyer how much they want to give me and settle for that.

I have always preferred selling to museums and institutions than to private collectors or friends. When the Museum of London purchased my large canvas, *Brixton Palm Sunday*, I dealt with a faceless but efficient accounts department and we agreed on a fair price. The same was true for all the museums who have bought my work over the years. There have been instances where I have donated a work. I donated all the unsold cartoons I did for *The Listener* to the British Cartoon Archive in Kent.

Even taking into account the factors of experience and ability, I still ask myself how a Francis Bacon painting is worth $142 million? And that's cheap compared to some pictures. The *Mona Lisa* is beyond price. So is *The Last Supper*, even if you could get it off the wall (it's a fresco). It always goes back to what I said earlier. A picture is only worth as much as someone is prepared to pay for it.

Marc Chagall avoided talk of payment and let his wife take care of selling his work. David Niven, who lived next door to Chagall, once told me that Mrs Chagall arranged a dinner for the potential buyer in such a way that she could see the master's reflection in a mirror but the guest couldn't. When the issue of the price came up Chagall suggested the sum by raising his fingers. One million, two million, three million, until he ran out of fingers.

16

NOVA AND HARRI

Harri Peccinotti, sometimes known as Harri Peck, was entirely responsible for making *Nova* the most influential style magazine of the Sixties. It replaced *Town* as the magazine that would not only carry in-depth stories about the latest trends in fashion, political thinking and people in the news, but present them in a format that broke all the rules. Put simply, a layout that took the reader by surprise. Typefaces that had never been seen. Artwork used in a way that had not been used before. Harri Peccinotti personified the unconventional.

When I met Harri he was thirty-four and I was twenty-six. He had a beard that went down to his chest, dressed like a French merchant seaman, lived in a sprawling farmhouse on the fringes of Surrey and Kent and gave supper to anyone who was passing. The food was laid out like a banquet and you might help yourself to either a boiled egg in its shell or a slice of salami or a chicken leg or a plate of pasta. His wife Gillian was a petite, attractive, warm and gentle woman who did a lot of the cooking. Although Harri did his share and was good at it. His guests sat wherever they wanted on whatever they could find while Harri sat at the head of the table in a Thirties dentist's chair. If Harri had a single button-down bone in his body I never saw it.

One day Harri called by and said he was on the lookout for a typeface for the *Nova* logo. Ralph Steadman was living with me at the time. He had left his family and was thinking about getting divorced. Ralph loved collecting odd bits and pieces, and earlier that day had been looking through *Exchange*

& Mart where he'd seen that a printer who specialised in Victorian wooden typefaces had gone bust and was selling his entire stock. He told Harri he'd go and take a look and that maybe there would be a typeface he could use. Later Ralph and I drove to the printer's, which was near Chelmsford, and bought the entire stock. Over a hundred trays in mint condition. The printer charged £25 for the lot. He told us that his grandfather had started the business in the late 1800s and printed only from wood type. Mainly posters for boxing matches and music halls.

Back at 60 South Side we divided up the trays and I stored my half in the Anderson shelter in the back garden. The following morning I called Harri and told him about the wood type and that there were a number of fonts that I had never seen before. I was sure that he would find something suitable for the *Nova* logo. Harri came by on his way home and took away as many trays as he could fit into his Fiat Abarth, which was later to catch fire when he drove it too fast up the M1. A week later Harri rang me from work and asked me to join him at the office.

When I arrived I found Harri searching through piles of paper covered with printed fonts taken from the wood blocks, most of which were roughly six inches high. There was one he liked a lot. The face didn't have a name so Harri called it 'Nova'. It was the one used until the magazine folded in 1985. It is now an established and very popular face – you see it everywhere.

Nova was published monthly and Harri would usually find a way of commissioning me to do an illustration for every edition. At the time only the *Observer* gave me more work. By far the toughest job Harri gave me was an illustration for a piece about the Prince of Wales (who had just enrolled as a student at Cambridge) written by royal watcher Kenneth Rose. Rose outlined the path he thought Charles Windsor would follow and the jobs he would do before taking over the throne. But Harri said the ideas Rose had were pretty dull and I could have six full pages and the cover to do my own version. 'The Six Ages of Charles,' he said. 'Do it like that.' And that is what I did.

The cover showed Charles as he was then, a not too bright student at Trinity, and inside I painted him as a naval officer and then as a racing driver since he seemed to like cars more than polo at the time. I painted him next as the director of a charity to save the Royal Philharmonic Orchestra, followed by one of him as the first royal to man a spacecraft. The last illustration showed him crowned king. The job was tricky because I tried to be as accurate as I could about the way he would look as he aged. To do this I studied photos and paintings of his immediate ancestors, who all tend to look the same. Perhaps because they seldom marry anyone apart from distant members of their own family.

Harri quit *Nova* in the early Seventies for a life in Paris. Although the art director who took his place was very gifted, there is only one Harri Peccinotti. You can buy books of his wonderfully eccentric and sexy photography in specialist bookshops, and not long ago Harri compiled a history of *Nova*'s covers and layouts which is available online. If you want to know what the lads in the graphic departments aspired to in the Sixties, Harri's book is it.

17

DARK HOUSES AND LIGHTS UP

Apart from Joe Orton's sexually open and farcically surreal plays *Loot* and *Entertaining Mr Sloane*, theatre went through a dull time during the Sixties. Pinter's light was faintly dimmed as was those of other Fifties newcomers John Osborne, Simon Gray and Edward Bond. All were writing fine plays and many of them have become classics, but the money was in revues. People wanted easy laughs, not serious drama, no matter how well acted.

A lot of theatres put on shows written by several writers. Cook and Pinter – in one of his lighter moods – both contributed to a revue that starred Kenneth Williams called *Pieces of Eight* that opened in 1959 and ran for a year or so. This was a long run for a revue and a reflection of how theatre audiences were changing from the middle-aged middle class looking for little more than a predictable whodunnit or drawing-room drama starring a pair of past-it matinee idols. By the time satire had established itself, young, hip swinging Londoners were buying tickets to see *Beyond the Fringe*, the four-man revue written by and performed by Peter Cook, Dudley Moore, Jonathan Miller and Alan Bennett. *Beyond the Fringe* opened at the Fortune Theatre in 1960 and ran to packed houses before transferring to Broadway, where it played until 1963. Again, the 'House Full' sign was out for every performance. I need hardly add that Cook, Moore, Miller and Bennett have all become part of the fabric of Britain's cultural heritage. Dear Alan's plays about homosexuality, Miller directing operas, Peter's genius, Dud's marriages.

But not all shows were straight satire. *An Evening of British Rubbish* was a mix of vaudeville, comic opera, *The Goon Show*, a circus, *commedia dell'arte* and a whole bag of its own tricks and surprises. It was performed by the Alberts. In the very early Sixties large crowds queued outside the Comedy Theatre to see the Alberts creating mayhem with the inventor Professor Bruce Lacey. In one sketch a deaf pianist has problems playing 'On Hearing The First Cuckoo In Spring'. When finding the Middle A key is stuck, he fumes into a crescendo of rage which culminates in him smashing the piano to smithereens with a sledgehammer. Finding a new piano for each performance would make the sketch impossible now, but in those days young couples had no room for a big upright piano in their sleek new living rooms. These unloved relics handed down from their Edwardian grandparents were dumped onto tips in their thousands. There was no shortage. It was fun at the time but in the years that followed we each felt a growing sense of shame that they had destroyed so many perfectly serviceable instruments. Me the most, since I was the one with the sledgehammer.

The Alberts were two brothers called Anthony and Douglas Gray. Genuine English eccentrics. They dressed in old military uniforms and spoke in an English last used by the Victorians. Dougie owned a Victorian mansion in the middle of the Fens. I once stayed there. It had no running water, gas or electricity. Dougie kept warm in the winter by never undressing. When it got very cold he invited his many dogs, cats and a goat to sleep on top of him. Dougie was very fond of explosions. One act involved him blowing up a full-size replica of a camel. It is thought his premature deafness at the age of thirty-nine was in some way the result of these nightly explosions. Tony's house, on the other hand, had a gas cooker, two wives and a lot of children.

I met the pair at the time the *Eye* was raising money to fight a libel action. Whenever we needed funds to fight a case we would do it two ways. One, we'd ask readers to send money and two, we'd put on fundraising concerts. Because Ingrams had always enjoyed a close relationship with fringe theatre he asked the Alberts to put on a show. Spike was involved because he had a lot to do with *An Evening of British Rubbish* and rightly took much of the credit for having discovered the Alberts. In the very early issues of the *Eye* you can see ads for the show with Spike named as the presenter. Spike was always a loyal supporter of the *Eye* and became a close friend over the years. Spike grew increasingly mad as he aged and hated the BBC more than anyone I have ever met. He would ring up the office and rant on for hours about 'those fucking bastards at the BBC' – and when the office was closed he would call me at home.

When we finally got the show together for the 'Great Gnome Libel Fund', to fight Sir Jimmy Fishpaste, it was thought a good idea if a member of the *Eye* staff who could perform could join in. This meant parts for Ingrams, Cook and me. Come the night, neither Peter nor Richard showed. I was given the part of the Indian fakir – I shall leave you to guess the way it was pronounced on stage. The role required that I cover myself with brown shoe polish, wear a turban and a dhoti, and walk over blazing hot coals (a clever prop with a red flickering light under the coal to make it look alight). In the sketch, I was asked if I picked my nose as a child. I said I did. I was then asked why I picked such a big one. Goon humour, I admit, but the gag got a laugh loud enough for one of the Alberts to ask if I wanted to join them on a permanent basis. They wanted to include more musical gags, which I could help with, and there would be places where I could add my own sketches.

Over the years we toured widely, and perhaps our finest hour was at a concert to raise money for Oxfam at the Royal Albert Hall. At the last minute the compere who had agreed to do the job called off (there was no fee) so I took it on. Paul Jones was top of the bill and Dudley Moore closed the first half. The Alberts opened the second. I introduced them dressed as the fakir and then Bruce Lacey came on for his *pièce de résistance*. Bruce looked uncannily like Sir Francis Chichester, the first man to sail solo round the world. He appeared naked on stage except for a tin bath which he wore like a skirt suspended from his neck by a leather strap. He circumnavigated the stage as if it was a flat earth with the aid of a telescope. It was a genuine show stopper, especially when the strap broke and the tin bath fell to Bruce's ankles.

Next up was the sketch that involved me destroying the piano. I began happily enough and there was much laughter from the audience of 6,000. But there was something I was not aware of. The wooden boards of the Albert Hall were very old (or were then). Almost a hundred years old. Nothing like a 20lb sledgehammer delivering heavy blows nonstop to the iron frame of a piano for ten minutes. It was too much. Half way through the pounding, the floor caved in and what was left of the piano dropped into the area below, leaving me staring into the abyss and doing my best not to follow. The audience loved it. The management were apoplectic.

Sadly the Alberts' life in show business came to an abrupt end following a terrific sell-out week at the Roundhouse on Chalk Farm Road in 1973. On the last night someone stole the tour bus which contained all the props and costumes. Everything. Hand-made, unique and irreplaceable – from stuffed animals to one-off musical instruments. Costumes and priceless props all gone. The Alberts never fully recovered and nor did the rest of the troupe. Even if we had had the money there was nowhere to buy the uniforms of the Raj or Norwegian foghorns. The Alberts retired not long after the theft, and those who performed with them, as Bruce Lacey and I had done, found other ways to amuse an audience.

I have made a study of noise over the years and was once a fellow campaigner with Spike to find ways of making people more aware of the effect it has on our health. Many came back from the trenches in 1918 deafened by noise – likewise, rock and rollers who spend night after night in front of speakers so powerful they can transmit sound over a mile are similarly affected. Noise at certain levels can affect the brain and has been known to be fatal. Peter Townshend suffers hearing problems almost certainly caused by a professional life lived with extremely high levels of noise. Research has shown that decibel levels are only safe up to around 70db. A rock concert is often in excess of 120db, almost twice the level considered safe. A small explosion is above 140db. A bomb is 240db. My guess is that blowing up a camel is somewhere in between.

CLATTERING TYPEWRITERS AND COW GUM

In the Sixties the *Eye* was printed by Leo Thorpe & Son, in their modest printshop just outside Neasden. Other printers had been approached but they were concerned about being sued and declined. The law states that a magazine's distributors and retailers, along with the publishers and individual writers, can be included in a libel writ. But being a very independently-minded soul, Leo decided that printing the *Eye* was worth the risk. He once told me, while lighting his pipe in the office one Press Day, that 'what these politicians need today is a good boot up the backside'.

When the pages were ready Leo came to the office in his old Austin van to pick them up. Sometimes his son would come too. Apart from John's white moustache I could not always tell them apart. John junior was younger by thirty years but the years didn't show. It's like that in some families.

Leo and his son did their very best to transform the eight pages and cover stuck together with cow gum and sellotape into a magazine. They had to photograph and reduce all the artwork and then stick the reduced images where the larger ones had been. The same was the case with the columns of type. It took hours and infinite patience. Luckily for us, they were professionals. Craftsmen. We were not. No one had been trained to lay out a magazine apart from me and the job was already in someone else's hands. Issue after issue, John's printshop battled with the clumsily designed pages filled with copy produced from a clapped-out Adler typewriter and stuck down any old how. What John and his son produced was

readable but not slick. It suited the content. A school mag.
Irreverent. Amateur. Perfect for the purpose it was intended.
To poke the Establishment in the eye with the sharpest stick
to hand. I liked Leo senior a lot. He was a good man and
honest. When the *Eye* got into financial trouble, usually as
a result of poor sales or libel, he never pressed for payment.
Sometimes he would wait months. You can write the funniest
gags ever but if no one prints them and no one sells the printed
copies, you are not in business.

Sir Charles Harness distributed the magazine from his tiny
depot in Wembley, a mile from John's printshop. Sir Charles
was not a real knight. He only acted like one. Like Leo, he
never demanded to be paid on the nail. While I saw John once
a fortnight, Sir Charles would be in and out the office all the
time, returning unsold copies and handing over the cash for
sales. He was a big man who always wore a blue suit, shirt and
tie. His manner was easy. Charming. It needed to be. As with
the printers who had turned us down, newsagents were just
as fearful of a writ. W.H. Smith & Son waited almost twenty
years before stocking the *Eye*. Eventually Sir Charles managed
to convince hundreds of news vendors in and around London
that, if the worst should happen, the *Eye* would bail them out.
Those who took a chance did very well out of it. In 1964 they
sold 90,000 copies. Combined sales of *The New Statesman*, *The
Spectator* and *Punch* didn't come close.

Sir Charles also did well out of the *Eye* and did even
better when the pornography laws were changed, allowing
explicit sexual content to be sold openly. As with the change
in betting laws, the freedom to sell porn (albeit, at that
point, soft porn) was clearly bound up with the notion of
the Swinging Sixties. The frenzy of a social revolution that

touched everyone, including high-court judges and cabinet ministers. Sir Charles was quick to spot the market and cleaned up. I for one was delighted that he made a few bob and more as a result of Parliament throwing out a law which criminalised harmless acts of self-pleasure. Moreover, as Peter Cook was forever at pains to point out, you could buy *Health and Efficiency* anywhere, a magazine that presented itself as an innocent addition to the naturalist's lifestyle that was full of naked children. It was Sir Charles who first pointed out how a strong cover would add to sales. His man on the spot would tell him, 'Not funny, Chas. Can't shift it.'

I am sometimes asked when discussing the *Eye* if I have a favourite cover. The one that always springs to mind is Macmillan on a grouse shoot telling his ghillie, 'Funny, I thought Jack Profumo was lying when he first told me it was true.'

From 1963 to 1970 I drew over forty covers. The artwork for most of them has disappeared. All drawings, cartoons and other artwork were stored in a large cardboard box on a shelf by the entrance to the main room, open to anyone who came into the office. Visitors from the postman to any old nutter trying to convince the editor that his father was Winston Churchill (more frequent than you would credit) could help themselves.

The *Eye* office today is very different from the shabby rooms we occupied in Greek Street. Like all offices now, computers are used for everything. And after over fifty years it is inevitable that some gags have a familiarity about them. That is the downside of satire. You can only be funny if the people you attack are worth the effort. Until very recently the Establishment has appeared dull and faceless and one might say some of the jokes with it. But the political and social climate has changed and the *Eye* has responded. The circulation has never been higher.

At *Private Eye*'s fiftieth anniversary bash, Ingrams took to the stage to complain about the changes Ian had introduced. He spoke of hacks sitting silently tapping their keyboards. There were phones but they never rang. Ingrams bemoaned the passing of the age of clattering typewriters and the heady smell of cow gum. The *Eye* is now laid out onscreen. Then, on Press Monday someone presses a key and the pages are sent via a satellite to a printer somewhere in the West Country. The mag goes on sale the next morning. The operation is highly efficient. No one takes eight scruffy pages in an Austin van to Neasden. No one delivers the magazine around the City in a clapped-out Transit. And no one marries the secretary.

19

RALPH AND GERRY

Before Ralph Steadman left his family and took the spare bed at 60 South Side he lived in a large house in Putney that had a large garden that ran down to the Thames. The gardens to these houses were so large that the electronic music composer who lived next door built a huge recording studio in the middle and still had room for fruit trees. This was 1964. It was a difficult time for Ralph. He had three young children, the youngest being less than a year old. It hurt him a lot planning a divorce from a family he loved but, for reasons he never said, felt unable to live with. And in spite of always trying to be cheerful it was clear he was deeply unhappy. He drank tea in the way chain smokers smoke. I once noted he put away over twenty cups in a single morning. Compulsive. The studio was awash with half-drunk cups of tea. But not any old tea. Ralph drank a brew he concocted himself, made from half Earl Grey, half Lyons Red Label. I recommend it.

When you see Ralph working you know he needs a lot of space because he draws large. On really big sheets of paper. The biggest they sell. So I gave him the bigger half of the studio in which to draw his attacks on the Tories and everyone else who represented right-wing authority. Ralph had been brought up in Wales and his parents were what was known then as lower-middle-class. He was quite mild until he picked up his pen. Then he got angry. Pen and ink were his release. Like Dr Jekyll's serum. One dip of the pen into the ink and he was transformed into the Spokesman for the Underdog, the People's Penman, the Scourge of the Rich etc. A lot of

Ralph's anger expressed itself visually in ink-splattered pages and drawings of dog shit everywhere. When Ralph got really angry he smashed the nib of his pen in the paper, which caused the ink to splatter. Ralph also smoked roll-ups. In a serious bout of rage Ralph could half drink ten cups of tea, smoke twenty cigarettes and smash a dozen pen nibs.

In the mid-Sixties Ralph was one of Britain's (possibly the world's) duo of leading political cartoonists cum illustrators. The other was Gerald Scarfe. And there are some who, looking at Ralph and Gerry's early work, find it difficult to distinguish between them. This is hardly surprising since both artists had little formal art school training, although Gerry will say he had. As a result, both developed their styles from studying the works of the French illustrator André François and the great American artist Saul Steinberg. Born in Romania in 1914, Steinberg studied architecture in Milan before going first to South America and then to the north. If asked, I will say I consider Steinberg to be the greatest draughtsman ever to have lived and that his visual imagination has no equal – Picasso included.

As if by fate, both Ralph and Gerry met in their early twenties when they enrolled at the East Ham Technical College. They had gone there to learn how to draw. I did ask Gerry once why, when he had already been a student at St Martins. As so often when you asked Gerry something he had no intention of answering, his reply came in the form of a chuckle. Enigmatic, Gerry. Always has been. Never knew from one minute to the next what he'd come up with.

From the East Ham night school Gerry and Ralph went on to get their work published, first in *Punch* and then *Private Eye*. Ralph was also heavily influenced by the *Daily Express* cartoonist and pig farmer known simply as 'Giles'. Ralph signed his early works 'Stead' in the same style but did not go so far as creating a cosy working-class family with an old granny and not very funny captions. Ralph added 'man' as he grew more famous and then his first name when he grew very famous. This followed his association with the crazed American journalist Hunter S. Thompson, who shot himself in 2005.

Ralph was generous and good company in the time I knew him well. He cared about social injustice and was able to successfully transfer his skills into award-winning children's books and visual accounts of the lives of Leonardo da Vinci and Sigmund Freud. He drove an old Morris Traveller and the latest styles never bothered him. By contrast, Gerry was always in the groove and went in for appearances. He was distant. He was not easy to know, and under the chuckle there is a violent temper that comes out in all sorts of ways. From the earliest days he always drove the fastest car he could afford. When he landed a high-paid job as cartoonist for the *Daily Mail* Gerry bought a top-of-the-range sports car and took me and a couple of chums for a spin. The Piccadilly Underpass is less than a quarter of a mile yet Gerry hit ninety all the way. I can still smell the burnt rubber.

Whereas Gerry has not moved from drawing faces with big ears and long noses (plus a huge signature) Ralph has matured. He has given himself new challenges, and every now and then you see a glint of brilliance. When Ralph ended his spell at 60 South Side he left me a cat. I called her Sadie, the name my grandmother gave my mother. When Ralph remarried it was the name he gave his daughter.

20

TRIPPING IN EPSOM

When I got a job working in the recording studio at Southern Music I met a lot of groups that had been cobbled together in the hope of getting a record deal and a crack at the number one spot. The really big groups like the Beatles, Stones and Kinks never recorded at Southern's studios. The Beatles recorded at Abbey Road, the Stones at Decca and the Kinks at Pye. The groups who used the studio at Southern were on their way up. Not top of the bill. They were, in the main, musically rough. Only a handful could play their instruments above the level of competence and in some cases not at all.

Of all the groups I met who were musically hapless, none came even close to the Dave Clark Five. It was commonly accepted that Dave and his mates had been assembled to offer a challenge to the Mersey Sound. Known as the Tottenham Sound, 'drummer' Dave hired some proper musicians to make his records and then went on tour with his Five, appearing on stage as if playing.

Dave was a nice enough fellow to meet, and when not miming he would talk happily about football and life in general. He had a spiv's nose for the main chance and plenty of Tottenham banter to pull off a deal when it came his way. The fact that he had the skill to make the most from nothing is what a lot of people did in the Sixties. It was certainly the case with the Dave Clark Five. All they needed was a set of band jackets and a song without much more than a dull beat and a chorus that everyone would easily remember.

Although many of the groups who passed through the studios at Southern were not much above average musically speaking, every now and then someone would stand out. Graham – we only knew him by his first name – was a singer and songwriter who was genuinely gifted. He had a beautiful voice with a near three-octave range. Graham played the guitar and piano and wrote his own material. He didn't have a group and wanted to make it as a solo performer.

Even though groups were the thing, a number of solo artists like Tom Jones and Gene Pitney were regularly topping the charts. Even jazz clarinettists had hits. Acker Bilk's 'Stranger On The Shore' made number one in the States. Until Acker's moody masterpiece, no UK instrumental single had even been near the top. But Graham did not have the looks. Or the personality. Or a press agent. And he suffered a speech defect that only left him when he sang. The reality is that rock and roll is the package. The looks and the music.

Graham has kept in touch off and on. The last time we wrote to each other he told me he was still singing. Weekends in a pub. He had no regrets that he never made the charts and was happy enough that he had been blessed with perfect pitch, could play an instrument well and had a voice that people genuinely liked listening to. Graham is the very best of the Sixties personified. Talented, original and happy to leave his ego at home.

'Glad All Over', Dave's big hit is sung by Crystal Palace supporters to this day. Says it all.

For a lot of the mid-Sixties I spent a couple of days each week writing songs at Southern Music in Denmark Street. I got the job through my work on my telly show, *A Whole*

Scene Going. I took a call on the studio floor one Wednesday afternoon during rehearsal from a man who introduced himself as Peter Eden. He said he was a music and pop star agent and asked me if I could sing, but added that it didn't matter if I couldn't because his partner Geoff Stephens was a songwriter who had written dozens of hits like 'Tell Me When' and 'The Crying Game' and they would get someone to make a record, put my name on the label and because I was on the telly I would sell millions. I told Pete I didn't need anyone to write or sing for me as I could do it myself, and Pete said that was great and if I came to his office the next day he would get me a songwriting contract fixed up with his associates at Southern Music, I would get an advance, and he and Geoff would be my managers.

So I went and met Pete and Geoff and got myself a record contract with an advance of £200, which was nothing, and I said so. The reply was that with the plans they had for me, Pete and Geoff could see me banking hundreds of thousands. I had only to look at their other clients. Mike Berry was never out of the Top Ten. I wasn't fooled but the punt was too good to pass over.

There was a recording studio in the basement of Southern Music where the publishers made demos. All the big-name session players would be in the building at some time or another and you got to know them when they recorded demos of your songs. Jimmy Page was often in the sessions and we got to talk a lot between takes. We both had similar tastes as we were both former art students who were self-taught musicians. Jimmy had been a student at Sutton Art College. I told him once that I was getting nowhere writing out-and-out pop songs for bands like the Hollies and Freddie and the

Dreamers and wanted to write songs closer to the work I did in other disciplines like satire and jazz and Pop Art, and he said he felt pretty much the same way. Then he said, 'I do a lot of recording at my home. Why not bring some songs over and we can work on them together?'

What people liked about Jimmy, as well as his brilliance as a guitarist, was his generous spirit. On a session, nothing was ever too much for him. He'd want it right. Forget the clock and studio time.

Sometime later I drove out to where he lived with his mother on Miles Road in Epsom and arrived just as she had finished work. Later, I think she said she was a doctor's assistant, or maybe a teacher. Jimmy was a very pretty young man with curly dark hair and little-girl lips and shiny eyes but his mother was more than pretty. A lot more. I guess she was about forty years old when I met her that sunny afternoon and she was the most beautiful woman I'd seen in a very long time. She was beautiful in the way Hollywood actresses were beautiful. Not the obvious vamps like Rita Hayworth and Ava Gardner. More like Gloria Grahame or Joan Fontaine. Jimmy was sweet and very polite, and his mother was even more so. She told me to make myself at home and made tea and got some fresh cream cakes from somewhere and then said she had to go out and would leave us young men to get on with our recording.

Jimmy used the lounge as a recording studio at home. It was a typical suburban room with heavy leather armchairs and a sofa. There was a table covered in a damask cloth with a bowl of fruit placed centre, and along one wall was a bookcase full of readable books and next to it a radiogram with a stack of albums piled up by the side. Not all were rock and roll. Jimmy and his mum both had a taste for the classics. Bach. Beethoven. Chopin.

Jimmy set up his Grundig tape recorder and plugged his guitar into his amp. Because he didn't have a drum kit, just a bass drum pedal, we used it to beat against the side of his mother's leather armchair. In the early days of recording no one recorded a full drum kit. The sound waves were so great they knocked the needle off the recording disc. They just used wooden blocks. If a drummer didn't have a bass drum, they'd use a leather suitcase turned upright and attach it to a bass drum pedal. It is a trick you see a lot of street drummers use today. And when doctored on tape, you would never know the difference. And there isn't any. A drum is a skin covering a hollow . . . er . . . drum.

I had brought about a dozen songs and we picked out the three strongest in terms of hit material. Jimmy figured that would take us to the early evening and be more than enough for one session. The first of the three was called 'Too Many Lies'. Jimmy took a sheet of paper and transposed the key, saying A minor was better than D minor if he was going to sing. I was happy enough. The key change made no difference when playing an armchair. We were about half way through laying down the rhythm track when the doorbell rang. Jimmy switched off the machine. 'I asked Jeff to drop by,' he said. 'He lives down the road.' He then went to open the front door.

Jimmy came back followed by Jeff Beck and his guitar. Jimmy introduced me and handed Jeff a lead sheet of what we were recording. 'You can play the solo if you want,' he said. Jeff lit a cigarette and glanced over the songs. If he was impressed he didn't show it. All the time I knew Jeff Beck his face rarely gave a lot away. What it gave, when it gave anything at all, was mild contempt.

Geoffrey Arnold Beck is a very fine musician. But I always felt he was one of those people who would laugh behind your back or snigger if you played a wrong chord. Or a wrong note. Or didn't act cool. A hard man to warm to. Nevertheless he was devoted to guitars, both playing them and making them from old cigar boxes and bits of wood, which he did as a teenager before studying at Wimbledon Art School.

Jeff opened his case and took out his Fender Stratocaster (not a guitar you can make yourself). With the cigarette still in his mouth he mumbled that he wanted an 'A'. Jimmy gave him one and Jeff tuned up. We recorded a couple of songs and Jimmy was pleased with the result. While Jimmy was sorting out the next song Jeff said casually, 'I've got some acid stashed in my guitar case. Why don't we take a break, drop it on some sugar and see what happens?'

None of us had ever taken LSD. I looked at Jimmy. Jimmy looked at Jeff. Jeff dug around amongst his packets of spare strings and other stuff and picked out a manila envelope. I said I was happy with booze, and maybe just now and then a smoke, but Jimmy said he'd like to try. Jeff told him to get some sugar cubes and they both went up to Jimmy's bedroom while I stayed down in the living room with the half-finished songs, less-than-fresh cakes and cold tea.

I guess they started messing around with the LSD because I hung around for a couple of hours until Jimmy's mother came home and asked me why I was alone. I told her Jeff and Jimmy were doing some editing in his bedroom and she smiled and made me another cup of tea and some cheese sandwiches.

It took me a long time to forget Mrs Page's smile. Even now I sometimes think of Jimmy's beautiful mum and even more often about what happened to the tapes of my songs played by Jimmy Page, Jeff Beck and a guy on the sofa.

21

PORTRAIT OF GILL

In 1963 Jane Asher shared a flat in Chelsea with Gill Brooke, who was my girlfriend at that time. Jane was very shy and sat around all day waiting for the phone to ring. Her black stockings always had ladders in them. She had pale skin and a lot of freckles and wore her lovely Titian-coloured hair long and wild. Her father was a consultant and her mother a big noise at the London Guildhall of Dramatic Arts. Gill's parents were from Middlesborough, and her mother was a maid and her father worked as a chef in a Park Lane hotel. Compared to Gill, with her high cheekbones, jet black hair and deep brown almond eyes, to me at least, Jane's beauty seemed a little wan. But there can be no doubt that, at nineteen, Jane was beautiful. One day the phone rang and Jane got offered a part in *Alfie*.

Gill worked at the *Eye*, which is where we met. She got turned down for the job of tea girl at her first interview because she wore her dark hair back-combed along with heavy black eye make-up and a short skirt. Everyone at the *Eye*, apart from me, was from the upper class. Gill clearly was not. She looked like Elizabeth Taylor playing Cleopatra. Gill reapplied for the job under a different name and turned up for the interview wearing a blonde wig, no eye-liner and a twin set. She got the job. About a month later she owned up, but by that time everyone liked her because she could type fast and make great tea. Wig or no wig.

Before her job at the *Eye*, Gill had studied French at the Sorbonne where she got the equivalent of a first class degree, a C1. And although we lived together she had a morbid fear her mother would find out. Mrs Brooke was a small bad-tempered woman who hated me on sight. She knew what my game was and no long-haired soft bloody Southerner with his fancy ways was going to have anything to do with a nice girl like her Gillian.

To throw her mother off the trail, Gill rented a top-floor flat in a block off the Old Brompton Road as a cover. The flat was small and cosy. Sometimes, instead of sleeping at South Side, I would stay the night, along with a hamster called Smedley and a rabbit called Bunny. Gill genuinely loved animals, and I am sure if there had been more room she would have had more – a small pig, perhaps, or a few goats. Both Smedley and Bunny were free to wander around as they pleased. Bunny ate a lot of lettuce and Smedley had a big appetite for such a small animal, which led to a lot of shit all over the floor. The smell didn't bother Gill, though, as she was a heavy smoker and drank more than was good for her. If the flat smelled bad it was more to do with stale tobacco smoke and booze than animal droppings. Although I can still recall the smell of methane.

I also drank and smoked more than was good for me at the time and was in quite a bad way for a while as a result. I smoked cannabis, though, not tobacco. It was the new thing. Age and class didn't come into it. Stanley Myers once told me that he had been invited to dinner at the North Finchley home of his middle-aged dentist, and when they had finished eating, his respectable Jewish host opened a drawer in the sideboard and fished out a pouch filled with weed. He rolled a couple of joints with the same skill he applied to drilling out a decayed molar and handed them around along with the port and mint chocolates.

My smoking and drinking came to a head the night I accidentally overdosed and passed out at the TV Centre after appearing on *Late Night Line-Up* to talk about, by way of coincidence, the effects of booze and dope on young people. After the show I went into a toilet and fixed myself up with a joint. Then I joined the others who had been on the show in hospitality and made the most of a bottle of Scotch. Then I don't recall a lot.

Around two in the morning a pair of security guards stumbled over me lying in a pool of vomit in the middle of a passage on the sixth floor of the Green Zone. I can faintly recall a voice saying, 'Christ, Bert. It's that Barry what's-'is-name from that what's-it pop programme. Better call an ambulance.'

When the ambulance arrived I was feeling a little better and told them to take me to Gill's flat. It was four in the morning when we arrived and Gill was waiting up for me, worried about what had happened. It was my twenty-sixth birthday and she had made me a vegetarian birthday cake out of fresh fruit. Smedley and Bunny no doubt made the best of the cake the following day. I could only eat a solitary slice.

Gill later became known for making Gill Bags. They were individually crafted leather bags which I decorated with Pop imagery such as stars and military insignia. Gill made her bags in yet another flat to throw her mother off the scent. This time it was in a large and very fashionable old Chelsea house on Paultons Square, which was owned by a much older man called George who fell in love with her. Gill made all the right noises and gestures so she didn't have to pay rent. George let the basement flat to writer Ian La Frenais, who, along with his writing partner Dick Clement, had become big names after writing the BBC TV series, *The Likely Lads*. Since there were only two TV channels at the time their very funny show reached more than half the evening's viewers, which was about twenty million.

In 1965 I painted a portrait of Gill to show in the RA Summer Exhibition. This time I used my own name, although I still used Stuart Harris for a lot of the work I did for the *Eye* around that time. When Richard Ingrams and Andrew Osmond, who was the founder of the *Eye* (he put up £200 to pay the very first print bill), collaborated to write a crime thriller (*Harris in Wonderland*) under the joint pen-name of Philip Reid, they called the hero Stuart Harris.

Richard asked me to do the hardback cover, which I did in the style of Sir William Nicholson's wood prints. (*An Alphabet* is a fine example of this style.) I still consider it my most successful book jacket. The figure in the picture is of a hunter about to take aim. As a reference I used a photo of Sir Alec Douglas-Home, the former Tory PM, who the *Eye* called Baillie Vass owing to his photo once being accidentally placed over a story in a local Scottish paper about an obscure baillie named Vass. The old Etonian was fond of shooting and spent more time on the grouse moors of Scotland than in the House of Commons, which many considered a blessing. Home's ability to do even simple things well was once demonstrated on telly when he explained the nation's finances using matchsticks. Baillie Vass's only qualification was a third-class degree he obtained from Oxford for modern history.

I decided not to aim for satire or a political mood in my portrait of Gill. I chose instead to include a number of visual elements that reflected both the style of the time and Gill's interests. To do this I surrounded Gill with images of Pop ephemera (as I had in *Nude Reclining*, shown the previous year) including a small portrait of Ringo Starr, a set of Polyphotos and cosmetic items such as lipsticks which Gill collected. When it was hung, *Portrait of Gill* did not have the effect of the previous year's hoax but it still attracted a lot of attention. In 1964 the whole world had become Beatlemaniacs, and anything to do with the Fab Four was guaranteed to get a mention. The picture I did of Gill got a full page in the *Daily Mirror*.

My painting of Gill in her Mary Quant blouse and purple trousers remains one of my favourites. There is a unique Sixties look to it. Up to date. Stylish. Sharp in some places and witty in others. Like Gill herself.

22

CREDIT WHERE IT IS DUE

In the early Sixties Beatlemania dominated the media and just about everything else in Britain. The only branch of culture to get near the coverage of pop and fashion was the cinema. And the box office hits were based on the books of Ian Fleming. Spy books. James Bond books. While it is true to say that the most successful character in cinema history rested on the powerful Scottish shoulders of ex-milkman Sean Connery, there were two other ingredients which were just as important: the titles and the title song. It goes without saying that a strong leading lady was essential, as were the locations, all the technical gubbins 'Q' handed out, and a credible villain. All important. But it is the opening credits that give a Bond film its unique identity. The animated sequence looking down the barrel of a gun in *Dr No* is a cinematic icon, as are many of the opening credits that followed. The credits for the earliest Bond films were the work of two designers, Maurice Binder and Robert Brownjohn.

I never knew Maurice but I knew and admired Brownjohn. I met BJ, as everyone called him, at the time we both had small parts in *Otley*, a spy caper written by Ian La Frenais and Dick Clement and starring Tom Courtenay. BJ played a tough guy because he looked tough and I was cast as a Chelsea layabout. Heaven knows why. We got talking during a break in filming and discovered that we were only part-time actors and our first calling was art. After filming was over for the day, at a location out of town, BJ invited me back to his flat somewhere off the King's Road to talk some more.

We took a cab. After a mile or so BJ said he was thirsty so we stopped off for a drink in a pub while the cab waited, and then repeated the action a dozen times before arriving completely smashed about midnight. BJ had a huge roll of cash and didn't even bother counting the notes he handed it to the driver. It must have been well over a ton.

Everything BJ did was generous. Big. Big as it gets. He was a large man, forty-two when I met him, but looked a lot older. He ate big meals. Drank whole bottles of Champagne or Scotch. Never a glass. And he was addicted to cocaine. The price of things didn't bother him. Having a good time and creating wonderful works were the issues.

BJ's flat was vast and sprawling. A bit like BJ. All the stuff he'd put in it was class. And comfortable. No over-designed sofas. No chairs that break your back the minute you sit in them. And all the walls, in almost every room, were lined with hand-built teak bookcases packed with books on design and illustration. Some were his. One is now considered a classic: *Sex & Typography*. That book alone is enough to place RB as one of the greatest designers of the twentieth century. Ask anyone who knows about design. They will tell you. And the walls that weren't bookcases were hung with his own work and that of designers he admired.

BJ's parents were British, but he was born in New Jersey and spoke with an American accent. He was considered something of a graphic genius as a teenager and studied under the great Hungarian-Jewish designer László Moholy-Nagy, who is thought by many to be the father of modern graphic design. BJ learned the art of designing credits using a combination of moving film and type from Moholy-Nagy. Traditional titles were often static, dull. Designers used a few tricks to liven them up, such as placing the cast and those involved in the production on pages of a book. As each page was turned it would reveal the various credits: composer, editor, make-up and so on. BJ changed title design for all time.

Single-handed, he invented a technique that was first seen in his opening titles for *From Russia with Love*. The bright jumbled lettering flickering over the close-up of a semi-naked belly dancer was revolutionary. They were praised as much as the movie, which is by far the best Bond of them all. Why? There are no daft visual effects involving spaceships and thousands of extras abseiling into man-made volcanos. No daft plot. Mr Big remains unseen and the supporting roles of Lotte Lenya as Rosa Klebb and Robert Shaw as the fake Colonel Nash are flawless. Sean was never more convincing. The exquisitely beautiful Italian leading lady, Daniela Bianchi, even with a dubbed voice, was perfect. And it had BJ's credits.

It is worth mentioning that Fleming cribbed the plot and style of the movie from a 1952 film called *Diplomatic Courier*. You can see it on YouTube. It has a train fight, an agent swap and Tyrone Power could pass for Connery. He even wears the same sort of short-brimmed hat. *Sinister Errand*, the book on which the movie was based, was written by Fleming's old pal Peter Cheyney in 1945. Ten years previously. Long enough to be forgotten by the time *From Russia with Love* appeared.

The effect of having created these titles was like having a massive hit record. It made BJ a star. He went on to do hundreds of brilliant designs, including the Stones' *Let It Bleed* cover (I have recently learned that the circular cake in the items stacked on the timetable was baked by Delia Smith) but the opening titles of *From Russia with Love* remain for me and many BJ's finest hour – or finest two minutes and fifty-six seconds.

When we spent time together he often spoke about his time in New York. BJ was a big jazz fan and knew Charlie Parker and Miles Davis personally. He didn't have any stories about them that I recall but just the fact that he knew them was exciting. To hear someone say 'Miles said to me . . .' Thrilling.

He gave me a copy of *Sex & Typography* that night we met and got stoned in his flat. Every time I open it I see something new. Like when I look at a Cézanne still life or listen to Schubert's *String Quintet*. He took design to a new level. Although rooted in the Sixties, the elements that make BJ's designs so powerful are timeless. That is how design works. A paradox. You are one hundred per cent a child of your time yet at the same time one hundred per cent a member of a tradition that goes way, way back to the very first man-made images. And reaches into the future. The same sense of space, line and balance BJ used for his posters and film credits can be found carved by an unknown hand on the lid of an Egyptian coffin.

Through knowing BJ, I learned to look more carefully at what are thought to be workaday designs. He knew that all design takes effort and thought, no matter what its purpose. Lettering for an ice-cream wrapper still has merit. 'Art Modeste' is now a term used to describe work that has a specific but workaday purpose, not something to be hung on the walls of the Tate Modern. BJ made a point of looking above the new cheap plastic shop fascias in streets to where the original shop signs were still visible. Signs made with care and great skill. BJ took pictures of many old London shops that still had legible Edwardian and Victorian signage. He once told me that great design is timeless. It just takes time to know it.

Cocaine killed BJ in 1970. He was forty-four.

23

MEETING 'ME'

The composer Stanley Myers had the palest grey-blue eyes I have ever seen. He was very quietly spoken and thoughtful, and had that way of making you feel that when you were with him you were the only person in the world who mattered. When he called you on the phone he said simply, 'It's me.' 'Me' was Stanley. Stanley Myers was 'Me' to everyone. We met when he was friendly with an actress called Gaye Brown who shared a tiny flat in Fulham with my girlfriend Gill and the seventeen-year-old Jane Asher.

There was always a bit of a queue for the only bathroom in the morning. Stanley and I got to know each other quite well, hanging around in our vests as the three girls got through bathing, fixing their hair and putting on their make-up. He told me that he had studied composition in his free time while doing National Service (there was plenty). He also said he played piano in the army band and his musical education was largely self-taught.

It was obvious to me Stanley was a serious composer and I felt a little awkward as I knew very little about classical music. It was also clear that Stanley had only a passing interest in jazz and pop music, which was the only music I understood from a musician's point of view. This changed dramatically when we became closer friends and then, a little later, collaborators.

Stanley lived in the basement flat of an elegant Victorian detached house with a large garden in the oldest part of Chelsea. It belonged to Rose Reckitt who was part of the Reckitt & Colman dynasty. I knew Rose when she was

Monty Sunshine's girlfriend back in the Fifties, when Monty played clarinet with Chris Barber and had a number one hit with a song called 'Petite Fleur'. It was the first time a clarinet player had ever made number one in Britain. Only American crooners and big bands like Ted Heath's who made records such as 'The Creep' and 'Slim Jim' for Teddy boys to jive to reached number one. Monty studied at Camberwell a few years before me and we got on fine, even though there was a twelve-year age gap. And that was also true of Stanley who was ten years older than me. Monty taught me to play clarinet and Stanley took time off from writing film music to teach me about sonata form and how to read and write music.

It was during this time that Stanley started to get really well-paid work from the movie industry and his reputation grew quickly as a composer who could provide a strong melody line. He wrote a score for a film called *The Walking Stick* which went unnoticed until it was renamed 'Cavatina' and incorporated into Michael Cimino's *The Deerhunter* in 1978. It made Stanley millions. He moved to a larger garden flat off Redcliffe Square, settled down with a lovely young blonde and bought a Mercedes convertible.

In the Sixties, well before 'Cavatina', Stanley was mainly writing for films with modest budgets that seldom found international distribution. One exception was *Kaleidoscope*. It starred Warren Beatty and Susannah York, and was a typical overcooked Sixties caper that gave Warren's ego plenty of air and, since it was filmed in England, a chance to add a number of English actresses to his very long list of what newspapers euphemistically call 'conquests'. Stanley passed the job of writing a title song on to me. Both words and music. He said that he thought I would do a better job as pop songs were not his strongest card and he never considered himself a wordsmith. Melody was his gift.

To write a title song, or any pop song, you want a word that has plenty of words to rhyme with it. 'Yesterday' is easy. 'Kaleidoscope' has four beats so there is nothing to play with. No beat to give you a word to take you to the next word of the phrase. And to make matters worse, there are only a handful of words that rhyme with 'kaleidoscope'. I found cope, rope, soap and Alexander Pope. No joy there. After a couple of days I ended up with this:

> *I look through my kaleidoscope,*
> *And sit and wait,*
> *And wait and hope,*
> *That one day, your face I'll see,*
> *A face that keeps coming back to me.*

I wrote it as a mid-tempo ballad and Stanley scored it for a small string orchestra, harp and horns. I went to the studios at Pinewood to record the song as Stanley had also fixed me up with a singing deal. But the session went badly. Too late in the day I discovered that I had no ability to croon. When the director heard the recording he paid me off and got someone to write a rock song that had nothing to do with either Stanley or me. They made the movie and released an album of the music Stanley composed, including the rock song. It is still available.

At the premiere in Warner's Leicester Square cinema I sat next to Brian Jones. A band had been hired to sing 'Kaleidoscope' on stage while the audience arrived. We were a minute into the song when Jones turned to me and said the song was shit. Then he got up and walked out. At the time he was suffering badly from drug and alcohol addiction. But he wasn't wrong about that song.

It was common knowledge within the circle of people who surrounded the Stones that Mick and the others wanted him out. His erratic behaviour was becoming a serious liability to the band's future. But Jones had a lot of money invested in his share of the 'Greatest Rock and Roll Band of All Time' and had no intention of letting someone else take his place. Jones got medical help, and it looked for a while as if he was on the mend. But it didn't last. Jones lived in Cotchford Farm, previously the home of *Winnie the Pooh* author A. A. Milne. He was found dead in his swimming pool at midnight on 3 July 1969. Jones, not A. A. Milne. Jones was twenty-seven when he died.

In one of the *Winnie the Pooh* illustrations, Ernest Shepard shows Pooh and Christopher Robin on a bridge throwing sticks into the river flowing below. At the time of Jones's death, the *Eye* did a wicked parody (drawn by Steadman, thought up by Ingrams) of the same image but with a dead Brian Jones floating under the bridge along with the sticks. A first-class example of Sixties satire was the general view of *Eye* readers. Bad taste was the view of a few who wrote to say they had cancelled their subscription.

Should you be wondering, the job of writing lyrics for *Goldfinger* went to Tony Award winners Leslie Bricusse and Anthony Newley. The film's producer, Harry Saltzman, famously said, 'This is the worst fucking song I have ever fucking heard.' He could have said the same about 'Kaleidoscope'.

24

OSSIE

During the Sixties there was nowhere in Clapham to go to socialise. The Windmill modernised and the trendy new pubs had no atmosphere. The only restaurants were Indian (the Golden Curry and the Taj Mahal – both still there) and there was a Greek working men's café on the Abbeville Road. It was run by a former hairdresser and his beautiful young wife, who could easily have been the female lead in a sword and sandals epic. She had copper hair and green eyes. Not the stereotypical Greek looks of Melina Mercouri but stunning all the same.

Since Chelsea was just over the river I spent all my free time on and around the King's Road. I would often go and have a drink in the Six Bells. At night they had jazz there and Decca had a mixing studio just next door. Jazz players, recording engineers and footballers all spent time in the Six Bells.

Peter Osgood would drop into the Six Bells for a few pints with a couple of his Chelsea team mates after training. This was around noon. Alan Hudson was one of Osgood's close mates. Ian Hutchinson was another. We got to know each other after a while. Peter was seven years younger than me. I was twenty-six and he was nineteen when we spent long lunch hours drinking pints of bitter ale together. Sometimes we drank shorts. Or wine. Peter also smoked heavily. And there were always female fans hanging around. Girls just about old enough to drink in a pub and have some fun.

Although born in Windsor, Peter was more like the

Cockneys I had known growing up in East London. He was sharp-witted. Put himself about. Drank hard and made it clear that he had no time for jumped-up managers who thought too highly of themselves. Sir Alf Ramsey never liked Peter. He didn't like Greaves or Stan Bowles or Rodney Marsh either. Too cocky. Too fond of their beer. Too clever by half. Not the sort of player to be seen in an England shirt, ignoring the fact that they were among the handful of world-class players England has ever produced.

It never failed to amuse me that when Alf was knighted for his services to soccer, he tried to elevate his lower-middle-class accent into one more suited to that of a sir. He made the common mistake of adding a redundant 'H' in front of an 'A' and thus would introduce himself as Sir H'alf. Those who did not find favour with him on or off the pitch shared my amusement. By which I mean everyone.

A month before the 1966 World Cup kicked off, I asked Peter to come on *AWSG* and discuss his chances of getting a game. On the show he said he was hopeful but the reply lacked conviction. Peter wasn't even picked. And it would not have mattered greatly. In the early Sixties, apart from the FA Cup, football was still a game for the fans. The man in the street wouldn't know a footballer if he bumped into one. But all that was to change on the afternoon of 30 July 1966. Thanks to a Russian linesman who thought the ball had crossed the line when footage of the 'goal' shows that it clearly hadn't.

The Great English World Cup Victory came slap bang in the middle of a decade filled with Union Jack mugs and mini skirts, and sent soccer to the top of the pops. Footballers were treated like rock stars. And they behaved like rock stars. They moved out of pubs and into clubs. Exclusive clubs like the In Club sprang up for the rich and famous. Located on a corner across from the London Planetarium, the In Club was the most popular by far. Footballers like Osgood hung out there. So did rock stars, jockeys, pimps and a sprinkling of London's mafia. Although I never saw him there, I was told that the club was owned by a businessman called John Bloom, an East Ender who had made his money selling cheap washing machines and even cheaper continental holidays. At the time of Bloom's rise to prominence, the *Eye* did a cover using French painter's Géricault's *The Raft of the Medusa*. From a dying man came a bubble with the caption: 'This is the last time I am going on a John Bloom holiday.' As far as I can recall, the In Club lasted less than a year before its fickle clientele found somewhere else to boogie. Bloom was made bankrupt in 1969 and, apart from writing a book in 1971 called *It's No Sin to Make a Profit*, very little was heard of him. He died in March 2019.

Sometime towards the end of 1966, Peter broke his leg. He was never the same player. Or the same character. The spark was gone. When Peter retired he opened a pub with his teammate Ian Hutchinson, but it didn't last. Either they gave away too many free pints to mates or drank too many themselves.

If you are passing Chelsea's Russian-owned stadium you can see a statue of Peter. There are two plaques. One large. One small. The large one reads:

KING OF STAMFORD BRIDGE
STAMFORD BRIDGE HAS MANY HEROES
BUT ONLY ONE KING.
GRACEFUL TECHNICIAN – NERVELESS

STRIKER.
ICON OF THE SWINGING SIXTIES.
ADORED BY FANS – SCORER OF IMMORTAL
CUP FINAL GOALS.
A BIG MAN FOR A GOLDEN AGE.

Hard to disagree unless you were Sir H'alf.

25

CROYDON PUNKS

Until the early Sixties Croydon Art College was little more than a suburban run-of-the-mill art school. It had a life class. A composition class. A still life class. And each used methods that had been established a hundred years before. And to be fair a few very fine painters had taught there – Ruskin Spear among them. But in spite of the influence of Ruskin and others, the vast majority of students left with a degree that carried little weight professionally and a portfolio of distinctly average pictures. And Croydon was not alone. All provincial and suburban art schools in Britain were much the same, saddled with teaching methods half a century out of date. But the arrival of Pop Art was to completely revolutionise the art world. It affected everything, including the tricky business of teaching it.

The trustees of Croydon Art College were well aware that art had moved on and were desperate not to be left behind. They appointed a former head of Camberwell Art School's Junior Department, Clifford Frith. He was the perfect choice. He knew everyone. Dressed snappily. Bow tie and neat beard. A twinkle in his eye and a charmer from top to toe. His remit was to restructure the entire school from top to bottom. Croydon was to swing along with everything else. Clifford's restructuring was simple and effective. He gave all the top names top jobs. Since Op Art had joined Pop Art as the in thing, Clifford hired Bridget Riley and put her in the prospectus as Head of Painting. He asked John Hoyland and Howard Hodgkin to co-found the Abstract Art Rooms.

The Print Room was given to Frank Collins, who had worked with the great American printmaker Stanley William Hayter in Paris and the Sculpture Department went to Allen Jones, famous for his glass-top tables balanced on life-like latex and plastic females dressed in S&M gear. The Textile Department was given to the legendary Enid Marx, who developed it into what was to become the finest anywhere in the world. Everyone said so. Clifford asked me to run the Life Drawing Department. Although I had no previous experience of teaching I told him I would be delighted.

Malcolm McLaren was one of my students. So was Jamie Reid. I didn't take to Malcolm, who hardly made an appearance, but I liked Jamie. He was bright and eager to engage in the new ideas I was presenting. But the majority of students were not yet ready to embrace them. My classes were a bit suburban-minded. Willing but unsure. One student told me that his father owned a tobacconist's near Thornton Heath but had never been or ever would go to London.

I decided that I would open them up. The very first lesson I took I told the class to go out to the newsagent's on East Croydon Station and buy a copy of both the *Beano* and the *Dandy*. They then had to choose a frame of a strip cartoon, cut it out, mark it up fifty times bigger and make an exact copy. A bit like Roy Lichtenstein was doing in the States. His blow-up paintings were not yet generally well known in the UK and not at all in Croydon. Most gave it their best shot. Jamie excelled. Cutting out letters from newspapers and turning them into headlines was his thing. It was Jamie who gave the Sex Pistols their now immediately identifiable visual style.

I started teaching at Croydon in September 1965. The first person I saw was Ray Davies. He was walking up the stairs to the canteen and I was walking down the stairs to the life room. It was a shock. We had said nothing to each other about either teaching or studying at Croydon. During the breaks we would meet up in the canteen and talk about what we thought we might be doing in the future. Ray was about to study theatre design and had formed a group with his brother Dave called the Ravens. We talked over the time we had met when auditioning for Hamilton King and how nothing had come of it. I said that I was still playing tenor and doing a little songwriting as well as my work for the *Eye* and easel paintings of heroes from my childhood. Sometimes he would play guitar and harmonica and sing while the other students ate lunch. There was not the faintest hint of what was to happen next.

When 'You Really Got Me' reached number one, Ray quit Croydon and got busy touring the world and we only saw each other now and then. Months would pass without a word. They still do. Some friendships need a lot of work to keep them going. If they are not right when you enter them they seldom become right. And sometimes the harder you try to make a friendship work, the worse it becomes. Then again, you can meet someone and it feels as if you've known them all your life. You don't have to say much or do much. Time and distance play no part. Such friendships exist in a world of their own. These friends are rare. Ray is one.

26

THE WIZARD OSMOND

When Andrew Osmond died in 1999 I wrote the following obituary for *The Independent*. I see no reason not to present it in full and unedited. My feelings have not changed.

Andrew Osmond was a writer of great industry who was blessed with a rich fund of original ideas. He wrote millions of words in his sixty-one years. Many of them have been greatly enjoyed and by an army of people. At his best, his writing in the genre of the political thriller was as good as it gets.

When Christopher Booker, Willie Rushton and Richard Ingrams (whom Osmond had met at Oxford) put together the first issue of *Private Eye* in 1961, they approached Osmond for funds. To their amazement he coughed up the then vast sum of £300. Although memories differ, it is generally agreed that Osmond thought up the name *Private Eye* during a meeting in Rushton's bedroom, which doubled as the editorial office in the early days. He then helped sell the first issue, wandering through Chelsea pubs and offering it to likely-looking readers for six old pence a copy.

What drew people to Osmond was his immense warmth and ceaseless generosity. There are few of us who are incapable of displaying some kind of charity, perhaps by lending something valuable or through a well-judged compliment. But, in Osmond's case, he was himself generous. It was not something he did, it was actually his nature.

There are countless examples of Osmond's generosity, such as when early on he found he had more *Private Eye* shares than he actually needed. His response was to give half of them away to those contributors who had none. This included me and my wife Tessa, who worked at *Private Eye* at the time. By extraordinary coincidence, Tessa received a dividend from the shares Andrew Osmond had given her on the day he died.

It often happens that generosity and a fertile imagination go hand in hand – they are possibly born from the same root. Osmond's seemingly endless stream of ideas was to serve him well when, after a spell in the Foreign Office in Rome (he had joined the diplomatic service in 1962) where he had met Douglas Hurd, the two men decided to co-write political thrillers. Their first was *Send Him Victorious* in 1968. The huge success of *The Smile on the Face of the Tiger* (1969) and *Scotch on the Rocks* (1971) was proof, should it be needed, that Osmond had all the skills to write professionally, and he had by then decided to go it alone.

Although well crafted and full of twists, Osmond's first solo novel, *Saladin!* (1975), failed to have the impact of the collaborative books. One reason may have been that he never told a story better than when it had just entered his head. He often put a novel through dozens of drafts, each losing a little of the brightness of the one before on the way.

I first met Osmond at *Private Eye* in the late Sixties where, having by now left the Foreign Office, he had been asked by Richard Ingrams, the then editor, to think of ways to help the magazine climb out of what had become something of a financial slump. For a while he ran *Private Eye*'s commercial side, which largely consisted of thinking up ways of selling mugs, tea cloths and satirical cushions designed by Willie Rushton. It was a job he enjoyed, not because it needed any commercial experience but because of his unlimited energy and enthusiasm.

The net result was a thriving mail-order business. When not being the commercial director (I name him this in retrospect as no one apart from the editor has any official title at *Private Eye*), he would spend the day walking around the office with a cup of coffee and a French cigarette, recounting in absorbing detail the storyline of a film or novel he had just thought up.

If it was a film, Osmond would go through the whole thing, from the credits to the dialogue in final scene. Some of his film ideas were brilliant and I suspect that, if there had been fewer, one at least might have got beyond telling it to the girl who dealt with the subscriptions.

He was strikingly handsome and always dressed with elegance and style, as well as being at all times exceptionally well groomed, even when drunkenly playing beach football in his underpants, as he did during one of *Private Eye*'s annual day trips to Boulogne. When he left *Private Eye* in 1974, he collaborated again with Douglas Hurd to produce *War Without Frontiers* (1982). It was well received, but a better book by far was *Harris in Wonderland* (1973). This was a detective thriller published ten years earlier, which he wrote with Richard Ingrams but under the pseudonym Philip Reid, a combination of their middle names. To collaborate on something as personal as a book is a clear act of giving, which is perhaps why Osmond's novels written with his friends had the edge.

Although he had been to Harrow and served with distinction in the Gurkha Rifles in Malaya he seldom mentioned these facts, though he used elements from both in his books. When he did speak about his military service it was always in terms of how hopeless he had been. In 1985 he joined Writers in Business and more recently he helped to form a similar firm, Company Writers, which set out to improve the quality of writing in company reports and the like. It provided a healthy income and was demanding work in its own way, even if it did not provide the challenge of writing a novel.

It was at home that Andrew Osmond's generosity came into its own. When he, his wife and their two small children, Louise and Matthew, moved to a large former vicarage in Swinbrook, near Oxford, they instantly became part of the local community which included a keen cricket team. Most people enjoy a weekend guest or two but not Osmond. His idea of a weekend guest was the entire workforce of *Private Eye*. Throughout the Seventies, the Osmonds turned summer Bank Holidays into cricket weekends and fed and watered (with Champagne) everyone.

Andrew Philip Kingsford Osmond, writer: born Grimsby, Lincolnshire, 16 March 1938; married 1964 Mira Stuart Baldwin (one son, one daughter); died London 15 April 1999.

27

LUNCH WITH THE RUSSELLS

Throughout the Sixties and for some time after, John Russell was the most influential art critic anywhere. John worked for *The Sunday Times*, which was the Sixties' Sunday market leader, outselling the *Observer* by two copies to one. The *Sunday Telegraph* wasn't in the race at that time, having only just entered the Sunday Paper Stakes. John also wrote for *The New York Times*.

There were other critics in the Sixties who were making names for themselves but they tended to have an axe to grind or pals to promote. Their insights lacked objectivity. The man on *The Times*, coincidentally called John Russell Taylor, was mainly a film critic. J. R. Taylor was well-intentioned but films are not paintings and his attempts to dig deeper into what painters do got no further than removing the top soil. He was eventually replaced by Richard Cork, a critic who only favoured artists who worked with piles of old bricks (Carl Andre). When a punter who was not a big fan of piles of bricks threw some damaging liquid over them, the Tate spent a small fortune having them restored. There were many who questioned how a pile of old bricks could be restored. I also wrote notices on art for *The Times* but not until the Seventies.

When John retired from *The Sunday Times* his job was given to an American woman called Marina Vaizey. Her prose style goes like this.

The charming, beautiful and even, at times, profound exhibition *Whistler and the Thames*, the highlight of the early winter season at the Dulwich Picture Gallery, is enchanting and absorbing on several counts: the interest of the contents in terms of aesthetics and of its views of the beauties of the working river, even in some of its subtly sordid aspects, and for subliminal questions about nationality and identity.

One very great painter and dear friend, now sadly dead, called her writing 'bogus'. I looked the word up in order to discover its original meaning. A 'bogus' was a machine used for making counterfeit coins.

Most art critics do not paint and are fooled easily by fads, fakes and trends. John did not paint but he had a painter's eye. He was an exception. He was not given to championing the latest gimmick or dismissing traditional ways of working because they were not fashionable. He simply looked at a picture, regardless of the reputation of the artist and judged it on merit. In the 1963 Royal Academy Summer Show my painting *Nude Reclining* had a wall more or less to itself. John told me later that it had literally stopped him in his tracks. He said he had been going to the Summer Shows for as long as he could remember and never seen anything like it. And there had been nothing like it.

What John and the public saw year in and year out were yawningly dull portraits of aldermen, bishops and mayors painted by the thirty-two members of the Royal Academy who selected what was on show and were free to hang as many of their own pictures as they chose. It was a cartel in all but name. The rest of the gallery was given to modest landscapes and a room filled with limited edition etchings, mainly of wide-eyed field mice and plant studies. All of which sold out.

John devoted his entire *Sunday Times* review to *Nude Reclining* and it was the only picture on the page. It was through this painting we got to know each other. John had been educated at St Paul's School and then Magdelen College, Oxford. He had learned his trade as an unpaid curator at the Tate, the gallery on Millbank (not the former power station) now home to a million sightseers. John was a mate of Ian Fleming. They met working in Intelligence during the war. John spoke highly of his old pal and I was always interested to hear his tales of their wartime adventures. There were times when I looked at John and imagined that his quiet manner, his charm and clear head would have made him a first-class spy, one that Fleming might easily turn into a character.

When I met John he was married to a former actress called Vera Lindsay. You can see her in *Spellbound* on YouTube. Vera was ten years or so older than John. She had a slightly beaky face with high cheekbones which might have been the result of her Russian/Jewish blood. Her manner was cold and distant. Aloof, you might say. The manner of many leading ladies of her time. John was just the opposite. As well as having the qualifications for 007, John had a very dry wit and was nothing if not warm and open. It seemed to me that the art critic and the former actress had very little in common.

As far as I could see, the Russells entertained a quite separate circle of friends. Vera's were mainly from the English stage and minor members of the aristocracy while John's were mostly painters. This difference was never more pronounced than the first time John invited my girlfriend Gill and me to lunch. John had been very complimentary about my painting of Gill in a review. He had also written about my earlier paintings. He particularly liked my portrait of Marilyn Monroe. John was kind enough to say, 'Barry Fantoni's portrait is better painted than Andy Warhol's and has a point to it.' I find this remark difficult to omit given Andy's universal claim while my work is now largely forgotten. After all, what is the point of writing a memoir if not, in part, to settle old scores?

Lunch was set for a Saturday in the spring of 1965. One sharp, John told me. Vera was very keen on sharpness. At least a week before, I began to anticipate what the lunch might mean to me. How, having John as a support, my paintings would reach a wider audience. The date grew in importance by the hour. Nothing must go wrong, I told myself.

The day was glorious. Trees were in blossom everywhere. The sun shone from a cloudless sky. Warm but not hot. A perfect day. I was ready by eleven. Gill was yet to decide which shoes she should wear. Maybe the new white PVC boots would match the purple skirt and lime blouse? Or maybe purple boots would be better with a white top? Gill had a white top but no purple boots. I was to go and get some purple shoe dye from a shop on Fulham Road. I could be there and back in an hour. One o'clock came and went and the boots were still drying. And so was the handbag which had also been dyed to match the boots and skirt. I called John and explained that we had been delayed. I told a lie, and as with all lies I can't remember what I said. John was his usual easygoing self and said I was not to worry. His wife had made a cold lunch.

It was four in the afternoon when we finally arrived. John and Vera lived in a grand house in Acacia Avenue. It had a huge garden and there were great paintings thoughtfully hung in all the eleven main rooms. Gill looked lovely in purple. She matched Vera's face. We went straight to the dining room where a large professionally set table was covered with lots of cold meats, a few lettuce leaves and, I think, a boiled egg. John had told Vera that I was a vegetarian. Vera told me as we took our seats that the egg was for me to have with the meats and the lettuce. I said nothing.

We sat down and Vera – dressed in Dior – scooped up some sliced ham and plonked it on my plate without saying a word. The egg followed. Reeking of ham. Not an egg I could eat. It was at this point that I said vegetarians never eat meat. Like slices of ham. I am certain that Vera had never met a vegetarian. Or really understood the word's meaning. John smiled and said his wife was certain she would find something. Vera half choked on a snarl and went into the kitchen. She came back after about three minutes with a freshly boiled egg in an egg cup. Spode. We left about five.

Someone once said that no one builds statues to critics. It is true, but there have been art critics worthy of such recognition. Berenson and John Berger spring to mind. So does Roger Fry. And I would add John Russell to that very short list. If for nothing more than his kindly manner in dealing with a vegetarian pop artist and his PVC-clad girlfriend who badly messed up lunch.

28

BIG DICK

Had I written this book fifty years ago I wouldn't have included this chapter. It is about my friendship with Richard Ingrams during my first years at the *Eye*. I have always called him 'Big Dick'. Others have joined me over the years. He has always called me 'Barty'. In those days he was a very private man. A man reluctant to express openly what he was feeling deep down. And his feelings ran very deep. All who knew him agreed. He was hard to know. And in spite of a biography running to 320 pages and countless interviews, Richard remains an enigma for many. But fifty years is a long time. I no longer feel writing about Richard is an act of betrayal, as I might have done earlier. Nor do I think he would see it as such.

When Richard and I first met, Booker was *Private Eye*'s editor, Willie drew cartoons and Richard was the contributions editor. But the titles were meaningless. Producing the magazine was a collaborative effort. Richard and Booker shared the only editorial room and Willie had a desk with his drawing materials in a corner. He would do his cartoons in the office sitting with his feet on the desk and balancing his drawing board on his thighs. He would mutter jokes to himself as he draw. And laugh when he thought them funny. And they invariably were.

Richard was alone in the office when I told him I would like a job. Booker was elsewhere writing jokes for Frost at the BBC TV Centre and Willie was learning his lines for that Saturday's edition of *TW3*. He took me for a drink at the Coach and Horses (which had just become the pub of choice) and we talked briefly about my plans and what the *Eye* would need should Willie move on to be a TV star and Booker think of another way to make money. On the way back to the office he asked me to do something for the current issue and said he would pay me £15 a fortnight. I agreed and went home and drew a Top Ten chart using a pop name for the painter and a pop song for his work. 'Sun Arise' by Billy Turner is one I can recall.

Richard knew a lot about painting and is a gifted artist. His son, Fred, is a highly regarded professional painter of bright, vigorous landscapes. In the very first issues of the *Eye* Richard also drew cartoons. They were simple, as are all the best cartoon drawings, and very gentle. Example: two birds are talking. One says to the other, 'Bed any good rooks, lately?' He signed them 'Ingo'.

During the early days, Richard and I often did things when not writing jokes. We might go to the National Gallery. Mooch around the Charing Cross Road bookshops which dominated the street at that time. And when he needed a new pair of trousers (infrequently) I would go with him. Richard wasn't good at buying clothes for himself. A lot of men who have been to public schools have clothes bought for them and Richard was no exception. They arrive in a wicker trunk labelled 'New Uniform'. Sandals and Aertex shirts were worn during the summer holidays. After completing the morning's jokes we would lunch at the Coach and then head down to St James to buy his new outfit.

This never took longer than ten minutes because it would be identical to the old one. Once the plain grey trousers and tan corduroy jacket with patch sleeves had been parcelled up, the tattersall check shirt placed in a bag, we might then look at some of the galleries in the area before returning to the office.

In those days small privately owned galleries often showed works by artists who had gone out of fashion. We both admired the paintings of Eric Ravilious and Edward Burra. And the cartoons of Pont. You could often see examples around St James and if you had a little extra cash you could pick up a minor masterpiece for the price of lunch at Simpson's.

Now and again Richard would invite me to spend the weekend at his home in Aldworth. I would take my paints and make pictures of the fields around his house, or do drawings of his son Arthur, who had just been born. I would also take my clarinet and we would play together. But only classical works. Richard is not a jazz player and my sight reading then was slow. But we managed a transcription of Haydn's *Saint Anthony Variations* after a few bum starts. We also got a little way into a sonata by Brahms transposed into a beginner's key.

At one point the office acquired a pinball machine and we held a weekly championship. Geoffrey Cannon, a pal who became editor of the *Radio Times* and oversaw its change from polite black-and-white weekly to full-blown colour trendsetter, sold them cheaply. The machine was one of the early models which was not in the least bit sensitive. You could use all sorts of tricks to get the ball to do what you wanted without being penalised. You could even lift up the bed so the ball went backwards before the word 'tilt' lit up. The winner's name would be pinned on the office notice board but since only Richard and I played it was a bit like Celtic and Rangers. Ingrams top one week, Fantoni the next. In later years the office pinball machine was replaced by the office piano. And again, only Richard and I played it.

Often Richard would give me a book by an author he suspected I hadn't read and thought I might like. He was fond of J. P. Martin's Uncle books, the tales of a millionaire elephant who was an Oxford undergraduate and spends his days in a purple silk dressing gown. J. B. Morton, who was better known as 'Beachcomber' and wrote the 'By the Way' column in the *Daily Express*, was also one of Richard's heroes. I grew equally fond of all the books Richard gave me but found none as useful as the secondhand copy of *The Reader Over Your Shoulder: A Handbook for Writers of English Prose* by Robert Graves and Alan Hodge. I think it was his way of helping me to write proper English, which I couldn't then and still can't. But at least I know the rules, even though I am not able to keep to them. Graves had his own rules when it came to marriage. He ran off with Hodge's wife.

The office at 22 Greek Street then acquired a record player and two records. Bach's cantata *Ich habe genug* was one. I am not sure of the other. It might have been something by Brahms. Richard plays the *Intermezzi* extremely well. One night in the summer of 1967 my girlfriend tried to kill herself. The following day I went to the office and told Richard what had happened. He said nothing. He got up from his desk, turned on the record player, and we sat in silence listening to Bach's cantata of desperation.

To know Richard Ingrams you need to look beyond his pale blue eyes. Look for signs that he is moved by fine paintings and Pablo Casals playing Bach on the cello. He cannot be bought and he has nothing to sell. He is what he is. You need to play his game and also play your own. Give and take. The blueprint of all friendships.

In 1968 Big Dick doubled my fortnightly salary to £30. And when I married Tessa four years later he gave us both a signed Sickert etching for a wedding present. A view of

Dieppe. He wrote on the back, 'To Tessa and Barty'. I can not imagine what it cost.

Recently we had lunch together and talked a lot about the early days and all the characters we had invented and jokes we had written – E. J. Thribb, Sylvie Krin, the ashen-faced Ron Knee and the much underrated attack on Heath's government, Heathco. Heath, who had taken the UK into the European Economic Community on the promise of cheap butter for housewives, was portrayed as the managing director of a manufacturing company based in a modern factory just outside Slough. Heath's pride and joy was the Automatic Plastic Beaker Dispenser Unit (APBDU) he had installed in the staff canteen, to be used for tea, coffee or soup. The staff represented the unions and did everything in their power to sabotage the APBDU, even though it meant they would suffer from not having plastic beakers. Unlike all the other parodies of prime ministers, Heathco was regrettably never made into a book. And given Brexit, no matter the final outcome, the issues with Heathco are worth finding and reading.

As Big Dick tucked into his lightly boiled skate and mash and I sampled the eggs Florentine we agreed that there was one short series we both felt to be among the most typical of our collaboration, and the best: 'The Bible for Motorists' by 'Old Jowett'.

The Prodigal Motorist

1. There was this motorist who had two sons. The younger of the two, Terry, was a bit of a lad.
2. One day he went up to his father and said, 'You're nearly sixty, Dad, so how about pushing a bit of

your cash my way. I mean after all it will only go in death duties.'

3. Well, anyway, they had a bit of a chinwag and Terry talked his dad around to his way of thinking.

4. When he got the money, about five grand all told, Terry was off like a shot. First he went to Jim Lumling's Sports Car Stable at Edgware and picked himself up £2,000 worth of highly-tuned Jag (only one previous owner).

5. Five minutes later he wrapped it round a tree off the M1 just south of Luton.

6. Of course, it goes without saying he wasn't insured and being only seventeen was not entitled to be in possession of a vehicle class A, C or F.

7. After he'd come out of hospital some eight months later young Terry found himself up to his neck in trouble with fines and solicitor's fees totalling a hefty four-figure sum.

8. Swallowing his pride, our wayward chum thumbed a lift back home.

9. His dad was on the roof fixing his colour arial when he spotted the lad coming round the corner.

10. 'Blimey almighty, it's our Terry,' he hollered, climbing down the ladder. 'Long time no see, son. You're a right turn-up for the book and no mistake . . .'

11. 'I've made a right Charlie of myself, Dad,' sobbed the repentant teenager.

12. 'Least said, soonest mended,' quipped Dad with a tear in his eye. 'I'll just nip in and have a shave and then we'll go and have a blow-out down the Steak House.'

13. Well, they'd just got stuck into a plateful of scampi with all the extras when who should come along but Terry's older brother, Walter, who had been doing a late shift.

14. When he saw the two of them through the window noshing away and boozing he got pretty narked and went for his dad. 'A bloody fine turn-out this is,' he cried in front of all the restaurant. 'There's me slogging my guts out down at the Post Office, bringing home fifteen quid a week and helping you pay off the instalments on the deep freeze, and what do I get? Not so much as a "thank you".'

15. 'Belt up, Walt, and have a drink,' said the old man. 'Your sour puss has spoilt more parties than I can remember. Come on, Terry, tell us a bit more about that lovely nurse you met in hospital.'

29

LAURENCE CORNER

When the Beatles got started a lot was made of their collarless jackets. They were the big thing. All the other bands had suits made by Moss Bros. The kind of suit a bookmaker might wear. But the Beatles' jackets were based on a design by Pierre Cardin. A tailor called Dougie Millington copied it. He and another now celebrated gents outfitter called Tom Gilbey made a lot of the Beatles' early gear. Tom was a member of the Chelsea Arts Club and he died in 2017. Over the years we'd talk a lot about the early days of the Beatles. He said that Dougie told him it was the other way round: Cardin copied him. Possible, I suppose. All that matters is that by early 1963 the Beatles' look was firmly established and millions of young men wanted it. And by doing so they saw themselves as taking part in the Sixties Revolution. Some wanted more. They wanted to sing like a Beatle and to act like a Beatle. I was one of those young men.

In the late autumn of 1962 when the Beatles entered the charts with 'Love Me Do', I was busy trying to look like, as well as play like, a cool West Coast jazzman. Like Art Pepper or Chet Baker. I wore my hair in a crew cut. I sported an Ivy League three-button jacket, a button-down collar shirt made by Arrow and a slim shantung tie with muted horizontal bars. Very cool. But as 'Love Me Do' turned into 'Please, Please Me' and then 'She Loves You', my wardrobe and hairstyle (and even playing jazz) seemed way out of date. So I had a Beatles jacket made for me by Lew Rose of Brixton and let my hair grow. I also got an electric guitar. Lew was a very funny man.

When a local racist climbed onto the front of his shop one night and somehow changed the 'L' of Lew to 'J' and the 'R' of Rose to 'N', Lew left it. 'Can't argue with that,' he'd say. 'I just charge all my *goyim* customers twenty per cent extra. Except the *schwartzers*. They wouldn't know a *yid* even if he was robbing them.'

The Beatles' look didn't last long and was soon replaced by the Carnaby Street look. Pseudo sports jacket, dark trousers and a pin-striped shirt. And there were military-style cord jackets worn with a black or white cotton polo neck. I liked that look a lot and when I went on the telly John Stephen would give me his military-style clothes to wear. He gave me a new outfit for every show and never asked for them back. You can see them in clips of *AWSG* on YouTube. Although it lasted longer than the Beatles' look, Carnaby Street clobber became a uniform and I have never been comfortable in a uniform. Not for long, anyway. It was due to something my father once said (a classy dresser when he had money). 'You want to get noticed? Look different.' I have a school photo taken in 1952 when I was twelve. Every one of Archbishop Temple's hundred boys has a short back and sides and his school tie in a neat conventional knot. Mine is knotted as a bow tie and my hair is set in a Tony Curtis quiff, thanks to the tongs of M. Louis, a fake Italian hair stylist who had a salon of sorts on Kennington Road. And although you can't see them, I have drainpipe trousers I made myself.

By the time *AWSG* was axed in the middle of 1966 the Carnaby Street look was nearing its end. But there was no obvious trend to replace it. If you wanted to dress in style, as I and all the other swingers did, the solution was either to have something made or buy unusual clothes from the charity shops that were just making their way onto the high street, or from ex-service supply shops. These clothes could be altered easily to suit your fancy. New buttons. A nip here and a tuck there. Bespoke is always expensive and not always good value. Even in the Sixties the cheapest Savile Row two-piece with four fittings set you back £100 (two grand today). You could get a small semi in Staines at the time for less. My solution was to buy from the ex-services surplus outlet on the corner of Hampstead Road and Drummond Street. It was called Laurence Corner.

When I was an art student in the Fifties the only cheap and durable clothes I could afford were army surplus. There were hundreds of these stores all over London after the war and most of them had an astonishing range of clothes and accessories. They sold everything from string vests to flying helmets. There was one on the corner of Granville Arcade in Brixton. It had a huge stock of German pilots' leather greatcoats. I got one for just under two quid and wore it throughout my years studying at Camberwell Art School. When it closed down I looked around and found Laurence Corner.

On one shopping trip I bought a pair of two-tone tan canvas-and-leather officers' desert dress shoes, which were unworn. A WWII American officer's dress tunic in dark olive with brass buttons which I cut off and replaced with a set of mother of pearl ones I got from Mrs Frith's Button Shop off Carnaby Street. (Mrs Frith was the ex-wife of Clifford Frith who ran Croydon Art College.) My shirt was ex-RAF and my socks were those used by officers in the Far East. Cool in every sense. My tie was standard army issue. A dirty mustard colour. I made sure I got a few of those. And I found a canvas army belt in a box which pretty well set me up.

It is not surprising the Beatles ended up buying all their gear for the cover of *Sgt. Pepper* from Laurence Corner. So did all the other pop stars – from Keith Moon (who I told to go there) to Boy George (who I didn't). After a while all the best stuff got sold and there wasn't much stock left in the way of genuine ex-service merchandise; all you could get were fake singlets and flying helmets. Then the lease ran out and the shop moved on. So did fashion. The new look was bell bottom trousers and maxi skirts that looked like they had been made out of Nan's curtains. Afro haircuts were also big, in every sense. I did a cartoon for the *Eye* at the end of the Sixties of a man with an Afro which completely covers his head. He is saying to his girlfriend, 'I don't know what you see in me, Gloria.'

30

SHAGGY WHITE DOG STORY

The two film-makers who quickly got in tune with the Sixties were Ken Russell and Dick Lester. Ken made films about composers such as Delius and Bartok, and the poets Dante and Rossetti. In 1970 Ken made a movie about Tchaikovsky's love life called *The Music Lovers*, and managed to get a shot of Glenda Jackson's ginger pubic hair briefly into one scene. I was at the premiere and among the many who later confessed that pro-Ken though we were, by and large, Glenda's pubic hair was possibly just a weeny bit gratuitous. It was a turkey and rightly forgotten. As was Glenda's pubic hair. Her career as a Labour politician was memorable, if for nothing more than her hatred of Thatcher. Glenda said on hearing of Thatcher's death, 'She was a woman who made virtues out of vices.' Enough, as far as I am concerned, to have earned her that CBE.

Ken was a big favourite at the BBC and he made a lot of his musical biographies for them. He was a serious man and on the few occasions when we rubbed shoulders, a little obsessive in his views. Although he became a Roman Catholic early in life he still managed to marry four times. By contrast, the American Dick Lester was full of fun. Both men were at least a decade older than the majority of the performers they worked with. In 1965 Lester directed a film called *The Knack* that now has cult movie status, which usually means not many people think it is any good. Lester also directed the Beatles' film *Help!* The poster showed the Fab Four standing on top of the letters H, E, L and P, holding semaphore flags that signalled the film title. I did a parody in the *Eye* with the signal changed to FUCK. And to think the *Eye* gets accused of schoolboy humour.

The *Eye* took a dislike to Lester and in one early issue devoted a full-page attack on him in its series called 'Pillars of Society'. They were written by Booker, who said of him: 'Lester is the first British film-maker of the age of Pop Art . . . He is a trend, a craze, a delusion, and his day will soon be over.'

A lot of the action in Lester's *The Knack* takes place in a large Victorian semi-detached house. The interior and all the contents of the house are painted brilliant white. Doors. Chairs. Stairs. Painting an entire house and its contents white was typical Dick. Apart from launching the careers of Rita Tushingham and Michael Crawford, *The Knack* launched white walls. White everything. Overnight, white was it. Today it would be the new black. Young marrieds and swinging singles all went out to their local DIY, bought a tin of white emulsion and got busy with the brushes and rollers.

The white paint everyone went out and bought was Dulux, a brand that was produced by Imperial Chemical Industries (ICI). Dulux was heavily advertised, which went a long way to making it the market leader. The ad featured an Old English Sheepdog. The ad ran for fifty years. The breed is now commonly referred to as the 'Dulux Dog'. I have recently discovered that fourteen different dogs played the lead – a bit like the actors playing James Bond (who got progressively worse after Sean Connery). My understanding is that all the dogs did a really good job and the first dog did just as well as the last one. Unlike 007.

ICI was based at Millbank, next to the Tate, in what was

then known as the Vickers Tower. The company employed around 30,000 people, which is the population of a small town like East Grinstead or Chichester. In the same way that small towns have a local paper to print news about plans for a new supermarket, a fire in the high street and a teenager being convicted of stealing a bike, ICI had a monthly magazine.

The *ICI Magazine*, as it was imaginatively called, was an expensively produced glossy affair and carried news about the company's new products, new plants and staff changes. You might read that Mr P. N. Billings was leaving the Runcorn development board to take up a new post in Slough. Or Mr Norman R. Rollings had just replaced Mr Keith B. Diggles, who was retiring through ill health. The management knew it was dull. So did the readers. They needed someone to jazz it up with a Sixties look. So they hired me to write and do cartoons. I have never had a harder job. And I have never been better paid. I earned more in a month from ICI than all my other jobs put together – £500 an issue – for what was, for me, a day's work at most. Eight grand in today's money. ICI had plenty. I didn't feel bad.

The editor who briefed me each month was called Francis Odel. We'd do it over lunch. He'd hail a cab and take me to one of a number of exclusive restaurants in Mayfair and talk about anything as long as it wasn't paint, chemicals and ICI. Short and slightly overweight, no one I have ever met knew more about fine wines and haute cuisine. His job did not interest him. Francis was a good man with a generous spirit, one of the brightest men I have ever met. Ideas interested him. He told me two things I have never forgotten or found reason to question. He said that originality was superior to intellect and if they found life on Mars it didn't matter unless it was intelligent. Francis ate and drank himself into an early grave.

Looking back, maybe the craze for white painted walls had nothing to do with Dick's movie. In the early Sixties holidaymakers spent two weeks a year in Spanish hotels. These rooms were white. All Spanish walls are white. Or the reason might simply have been the collective unconscious revolting against the grey postwar decade. One for Jung. In any event, a lot of people painted their walls white and the paint they used was Dulux. ICI is now owned by a Dutch multi-international mega-conglomerate worldwide multi-billion enterprise called AkzoNobel. I doubt they have a house magazine apart from *The Wall Street Journal*.

31

THE GOLDEN EGG

When you finished recording late in London in the Sixties there was nowhere to eat. The only place open all day and all night in central London was the Golden Egg. It was a modern building on the corner of Park Lane and Oxford Street, just along from where Primark is now. The Golden Egg was on two floors with horribly bright neon lights and served food on plastic plates and drinks in plastic cups. The tables were also plastic, as were the chairs. And cutlery. The menu was short. You could get egg and chips and a burger and chips. And they had ice cream and coffee and Coke. Unlike the decor, the food was surprisingly good. The chips were not frozen and the eggs were done to a T.

The Kinks recorded in Pye's studios just up the Edgware Road so when they finished a session and I was around we'd go and eat at the Golden Egg. It was summer the last time we ate there and the Kinks had just recorded 'Rainy Day In June'. It took most of the session because they had to mix the sound of thunder with the backing vocals and it took a lot of care to get the balance right. The session had overrun because Dave had gone missing for the backing track. The whole studio building was searched from top to bottom. Everyone was hunting for Dave. The security guards included. As it happened, I found Dave stoned in a locked toilet cubicle. I forced the door open and got the lead guitarist back on his feet and into the studio. After a lot of black coffee and pills he finished the session. I doubt if he'll remember.

I preferred to record late. So did the Stones, the Beatles, the Kinks and just about everyone. The studios had other work during the day. Film music kicked off at around seven. The afternoons were usually when orchestral music had a slot. Then pop and rock. At one in the morning the town was dead. It swung like crazy until the pubs closed at ten-thirty. The few places open were not easy to get into. There were all-night pubs by Smithfields and Covent Garden, and cab drivers' cabins but they didn't serve outsiders. Even Indian restaurants would pack it in at midnight. The fact is that Swinging London was to some extent an illusion and that, apart from a few boutiques and record shops, life was pretty dull.

But there were one or two places that were part of the new scene. Small and unobtrusive places off the beaten track. The King's Road had a couple of bistros that stayed open until after midnight: Spot One and Spot Two. The food wasn't special but the waitresses were some of the most beautiful women in town. Most were out-of-work actresses.

The place I went to most was on Walton Street. It was called Pierre's. The owner, who was also the chef, told me he was French. Pierre spoke French and we would speak French now and then. But I once forgot and spoke to him in Italian and he replied in Italian. Perfectly. His food was good, and because I am a vegetarian he would always knock up something not on the menu. Like his blood, Pierre's food was a mix of French and Italian. But he stuck to classic vegetarian dishes when I ate there. Pierre's risotto with wild mushrooms was perfect when wild mushrooms were in season. And the same goes for the lightly grilled asparagus with garlic, pepper and lemon juice. Dishes like these were hard to find in those days. He also did a risotto with summer berries, unheard of in Swinging London or anywhere else outside Italy.

Another big reason for eating at Pierre's was that his room would be empty by the time I got there. He'd cook me something and we would sit alone and talk, sharing a bottle of wine – usually white. Usually French. Usually Sauvignon. In time, I discovered that the reason Pierre closed late was because he was a gambler. He played cards. When Pierre finally closed for the night he'd go and find a card game. Lose. Get into debt. Borrow money. Win some. Lose more. The last time I saw him he said he was in debt. Thirty thousand pounds in debt. About a week later I turned up for supper and found Pierre's shut. There was no notice to say why. I asked the owners of other restaurants in the street if they knew anything but none had any idea. Most of them didn't really know much about Pierre. I can only guess his disappearance had something to do with his debt.

To this day I have no idea what became of Pierre. A year later his small restaurant opened up under a new owner who kept normal hours and offered an expensive and unimaginative menu aimed at businessmen.

The *Eye* carried a lot of ads for eating places in its early days. One that appeared in every issue was for the Bistro Vino. In a dining room no bigger than the average lounge, you could order mushrooms on toast or cuts of Scottish beef flown down daily from a farm near Aberdeen. There was no wine list; you took your own and you ate by candle light on gingham tablecloths. The Bistro Vino's menu was a mix of public school dinner and a transport café's all-day breakfast. The place was packed every night of the week and although the kitchen closed at midnight diners hung around till the small hours.

Michael Eddowes owned the Bistro Vino. He was a top lawyer who ran the family firm. It specialised in divorce cases, mainly cases brought by the very wealthy, and Michael lived well off both the family money and that which he earned himself. He bought a mews flat in Yeoman's Yard in Knightsbridge but he spent most his time out of court in his bistro. He had opened it more or less on a whim. 'As a hobby,' he once told me. When the Bistro Vino showed signs of being a success, Michael got a professional business partner to take care of the catering while he wandered around the tables making sure everyone's sardines and garden peas were up to scratch.

I would eat at the Bistro Vino on Wednesday nights after the telly show. Michael knew that I worked at the *Eye*, as well as presenting *AWSG*, and we quickly became friends. He was over sixty when I met him. He was a man rich with old-world charm. And wealth. Even when dressing casually, Michael wore expensive silk cravats, and you could tell his clothes had been hand-made. He kept what was left of his hair well groomed and when he spoke his manner always had the air of a barrister. It was if everything he said might easily be prefaced with 'I put it to you, Mr So and So . . .' Or 'That is for the jury to decide.' He was amusing company and he laughed easily. But Michael was never hearty. He was a man with a mission, and his mission came first. This was to reveal The Truth. Wrongdoers were to be exposed. The wrongfully convicted released and pardoned. The culprits punished. Lee Harvey Oswald was a case in point and became an obsession. Timothy Evans was another.

The *Eye* interested him. Not the jokes, but the pieces Paul Foot wrote exposing corruption, especially among institutions such as government, local councils and the police. Particularly the police, who in spite of their show trial-type internal investigations are not always held accountable for their actions. Michael firmly believed that many people were wrongly convicted of crimes they did not commit due to false police evidence. He could cite any number of high-profile cases to prove his point.

He said he knew for certain that Lee Harvey Oswald did not assassinate Kennedy. Two marksmen blew the top off the president's head – one of them from behind the hedge at the top of the grassy knoll. He was also certain that Timothy Evans, who was convicted and hanged for the murder of his wife and daughter, was innocent. And he was right. Serial killer John Christie was finally found guilty. To illustrate how far Michael would go to prove he knew the truth about Evans, he actually bought and lived in the house where Evans had lived. He told me that one morning he was shaving and Evans' face was staring back at him in the mirror telling him he was innocent.

Michael was also convinced that the fashionable osteopath Stephen Ward was murdered by MI5 when it was discovered that John Profumo had paid to have sex with a society girl called Christine Keeler. Profumo was Secretary of State for War at the time. Ward ran a high-class brothel when not attending to his clients' lower lumbar problems and stiff necks. Michael met Keeler. She thought he was looking for sex. He was looking for the truth. And he found it. He discovered that Ward's clients included cabinet ministers, members of the aristocracy, members (one) of the royal family and Russian spies on expenses. While having sex they all wore black eye masks to conceal their identity. It worked for some but not for all and the truth finally came out. Profumo resigned and Keeler and Mandy Rice-Davies became celebrities.

Mandy is in the *Oxford Dictionary of Quotations* for a reply she gave when on trial for living off immoral earnings. She said Lord Astor had paid to have sex with her. Astor's QC told the court that his client had never met Miss Rice-Davies. 'He would say that, wouldn't he?' was Mandy's memorable response. Christine didn't get into a dictionary of quotations but a photo of her sitting naked astride a chair made the front pages of newspapers and magazines worldwide. One of my favourite *Eye* covers involving the Keeler case was of Prime Minister Macmillan saying, 'I thought John Profumo was lying when he told me it was true.'

When I ate supper alone at the Bistro Vino, Michael would spend time at my table telling me about the way the CIA had framed Oswald and the police had given false evidence at Evans' trial. Eating mushrooms and toast, I didn't take Michael's views too seriously. Ask me now what I think and I'd say he was years ahead of his time. JFK? Does anyone today seriously believe you can fire three shots in succession on a single-bolt, twenty-year-old Italian Mannlicher Carcano rifle and kill a man in a moving car? Even the Warren Commission's ace marksmen couldn't manage it. Facts are facts. The world is not flat and there is no Father Christmas.

Michael Eddowes died in 1992 having spent millions to see justice done. He was right most of the time. Mandy died in 2014, Keeler in 2017. Her death made headlines and her former solicitor told the press: 'She was the last survivor of a story that gripped Sixties Great Britain and the world more than fifty years ago.'

Gripped it and changed it.

32

POETRY, JAZZ AND STEW

The International Poetry Incarnation, organised by the young film-maker Barbara Rubin, took place at the Royal Albert Hall on 11 June 1965. The poets scheduled to read were Pete Brown, William S. Burroughs, Gregory Corso, Lawrence Ferlinghetti, Allen Ginsberg, Anselm Hollo, Michael Horovitz, Ernst Jandl, Christopher Logue, George Macbeth, Frank Miller, Adrian Mitchell, Alexander Trocchi and Andrei Voznesensky. Pablo Neruda was booked but didn't show. Some poets, unable to get there for various reasons like not having the fare, sent tapes. Even more poets who were not invited turned up and hung around trying to find a slot to read. Since there was no running order it didn't matter who you were, outside the Big Names.

I was there most of the day. Over 7,000 people attended the shambolic mind-numbing dope-fuelled event, including the future prime minister of India, Indira Gandhi. There is a film of the event on YouTube. It was made by Peter Whitehead. *Wholly Communion* does a pretty good job of reflecting some of the atmosphere. Barbara Rubin was a key figure in Andy Warhol's multi-media Factory. Her highly praised film *Christmas on Earth* was originally called *Cocks and Cunts*. It shows homosexual men having sex. Her other claim to fame is that when Bob Dylan fell off his motorbike she looked after him. As a sign of his gratitude Bob put her photo on one of his album sleeves. Bob was big like that. Rubin's idea of putting on a poetry show was to let it all hang out. It was chaos. But she was fun to be with and her early death, aged only thirty-five, caused much sadness among her many friends.

I went because Michael Horovitz was a pal and he invited me. 'It will be a chance to meet some heavy American beats,' he said on the bus there. 'You can go a long way when you get to know some really heavy American beats like Allen and Gregory.' I'd first met Horovitz in the middle of Soho Square a month after Charlie Parker died. He was carrying the *Charlie Parker Memorial Album*. He told me he had just bought it but didn't own a record player but he knew someone who did and so he was heading down to Anton's place to give it a spin. Anton had a record player and was a ten-minute walk. He asked me to tag along. We would get to know each other and if I had any money I could buy him something to eat on the way. And if there was any left over I might lend it to him for a while.

Anton's pad was four rooms over a sandwich bar in Newport Place. The floors of all the rooms were covered with mattresses and bedding and there wasn't much else. The record player was under some books, under a pile of clothes. There were no tables or chairs and everyone sat on the floor. In the kitchen there was a gas ring burning under a two-gallon copper saucepan filled with what smelled like meat stew. The saucepan was the kind you see in professional kitchens, which is where it probably belonged before Anton got hold of it. Anton wasn't there. Others were. About a dozen men of various ages. Most looked like they were tramps. Others might have been painters – those who don't sell a lot. Or anything. Ever. One or two were dressed in clothes that fitted and no one took the least bit of interest in anyone else. As well as the smell of the stew, there was a smell of dope being smoked and stale beer and bodies and sheets that needed a wash and fresh air.

Horovitz got the record player to work and played his *Charlie Parker Memorial Album* about a dozen times and said 'yeah' every time Bird hit a really fast run. One of the others who was smoking said 'yeah' but not at the same time as Horovitz. There seemed to be a slight disagreement as to when Bird exactly hit it. Horovitz always spoke like he was reciting a poem, in a slow drawl with no rise and fall. It suited the poems he wrote but sounded out of place at other times. Back then he had a long black beard, a black overcoat, no tie and wax-coloured skin and pebble glasses. A rabbi, if you didn't know better. Aged eighty-four, he still speaks in a slow drawl. Some would say even slower.

After a while Horovitz stopped playing his record and the hepcat smoking the joint, which he didn't pass round as was the custom, used the gap to tell me he played alto. He was older than me, a lot older, and had grown a little goatee beard that was going grey at the ends. I told him I played alto and clarinet. He wasn't interested. Then Anton came in. Anton was a Russian with Polish and German blood and worked as an actor when he could but earned his living washing up in kitchens. Shift work. But he mostly worked nights and he also washed buses, taxi cabs and ambulances, and the night shift was best because it paid more. He was heavy-built and had fair hair cropped short. His small flat forehead ran down into a wide nose so he looked like a man who'd been hit in the face with a flat iron. His mouth was wide and his cheeks high and broad. When they wanted a German Gestapo officer they didn't have to look further than Anton. But because he spent so much time washing up he never got to meet the people who cast German officers.

Anton immediately got busy at the stew pot. While chopping an onion he began a debate on the nature of pain. Anton had picked grapes the previous summer in France and said it was painful. The back suffered. The heat burned. He said he could still feel the pain. Horovitz argued that it was impossible to feel pain in memory. Anton argued that remembered pain was still pain. But different. They threw names at each other to prove a point. Hegel! Marx! Marcuse! During the argument more men came into the room and ate stew and added their own voice to the argument. I would have joined in but up until that time I had only learned life drawing and how to play the clarinet and a few bebop licks on the alto. Arguing about pain and grape picking was beyond my world. I'd learn about it later.

33

MR AND MRS BLUESBREAKER

John Mayall and the Bluesbreakers are a living legend spanning almost six decades. Think of Clint Eastwood with a C melody blues harp instead of a Colt .45 and you have John Mayall. As I write, John is still going strong, but without the band. I am not sure what happened to the Bluesbreakers. I suspect they lived up to their name and broke up.

I met John through Eric Clapton shortly after we filmed Eric miming playing the guitar for the title sequence of *A Whole Scene Going*. It was the same time that Eric joined John's band. John had a really good ear for spotting talent. Over the years his Bluesbreakers gave the fastest guitarists of their time the chance to show what they could do. I won't list them all here because, like their solos, the list is very long. I think Eric was the first.

A jack of all trades, John played the guitar, the organ, the piano, the bass guitar and blues harp. He sang, wrote songs, made his own recordings, designed his own record sleeves, took photos of the Bluesbreakers for the record sleeves, wrote the liner notes and did the graphics. As far as I know he stopped short at reviewing his own records but he reviewed everyone else's. John built his reputation around the gifts of his lead guitarists. And the bandleader from Macclesfield was sharp enough to know it and make it pay. Clapton was the draw. So were Pete Green and Mick Fleetwood.

John lived in a vast Victorian detached house close to a railway station, which I think was Grove Park. It had a huge rambling garden. He'd lived there a while and done lots of renovating and building. He put in a recording studio, a darkroom and a design studio. He planted a vegetable patch and herb garden and took good care of the orchard. I think he may have had some chickens running around, possibly a goat, but I am not one hundred per cent sure.

Not long after we met, John invited me to a party he was giving the coming Friday. His parties were legendary for their length (many days) and the substances and booze consumed (tons and tankerloads). To be invited was a sign that you had reached the inner circle of bluesbreaking. It was August. Although the day had been very hot, by the early evening there was a breeze and, as all the windows were open, it was wonderfully cool inside. I sat on a large leather sofa and John was looking after the music on his hand-built sound system.

John had records from just about every style of music that was close to R&B and jazz. Some were extremely rare. Like the early Sun label recordings of groups who were known to very few local followers but had a B-side later recorded by Elvis or Little Richard. John knew everything about B-sides. And A-sides. He said his collection ran into thousands. But not all were music. He had a massive collection of humour records. He was a big fan of Lenny Bruce and had every album he made. He said he picked them up when he toured in America. I told him I had met Lenny when Peter Cook brought him over to perform at the Establishment Club. John was impressed. He had never met Lenny and asked me what he was like to hang out with. I told him he was a lot more fun on stage than in person. His drug habit affected his moods and you could never be sure which Lenny you'd be talking to. He was pretty miserable most of the time.

John pulled a Lenny Bruce record from the shelf marked 'Humour', which had all the records alphabetically indexed, and gave it a spin. The label Bruce recorded for was Fantasy and they pressed their records onto red see-through vinyl. The album was called *Lenny Bruce – American* and full of material I had never heard. Lenny called his material 'bits'. The album contained a bit that is among his greatest.

'The Palladium' runs for about twenty minutes and tells of a rising New York comic who plays the Palladium and fails to get a single laugh. Lenny plays all seventeen characters and, like nearly all his albums, it was recorded live. I asked John if he could get me some Lenny Bruce albums when he was next in the States. John was nothing if not generous and said I could have his collection. He would get some more the next time he toured America.

John's wife Pam joined us and gave me a glass of his home-made beer. Pam was very elegant. Tall with soft eyes and a warm smile. She said she had seen me on the telly and that I had a beautiful mouth (no one had ever told me that before and nor have they since). Then she kissed me and wandered off with the drinks tray. John carried on sorting out the music and said Pam was a very special woman. She had a strong will and did what she wanted when she wanted. He then put on 'Tired And Sleepy', a rockabilly single by the Cochran Brothers (Eddie and Hank, unrelated) and went off to sort out the curry.

Later on in the evening Eric told John that I played tenor and we talked a bit about my coming along as a guest. John liked the idea and we fixed it up. Then a whole crowd turned up, including a couple of Bluesbreakers complete with guitars. By midnight the house was heaving. And the live music was quality. The less formal atmosphere of a house party compared to a thousand-seater venue took the music closer to its roots, like the rent parties in St Louis and Kansas City. No one played better than Eric when left to amuse himself and not show off. Hendrix was the same.

More and more people turned up as the night became the early hours. The music was wonderfully relaxing and I don't think I shifted from the sofa the entire evening. I sat drinking, smoking a little, and looking through John's record collection. I drank a lot that night but was not in the least bit drunk when Pam came and said it was time for bed because the party was running over to the next day. I said I was okay on the sofa. I hadn't fully understood what she meant. She said nothing, just gave me another of her warm smiles and led me upstairs.

After that night Pam and I would spend time together at 60 South Side. Her views were way ahead of those of most women I had met, and I had known some pretty wild women. But Pam wasn't wild in any way. She had a mind of her own, as John said, and often penetrating insights. Without being in the least critical, she would tell me what it was like living with a man driven by his self-belief while at the same time trying to make something of her own life, apart from bringing up their four children. She told me of her need to be independent and not exist only as someone's wife, even if that someone was John.

They divorced not long after Pam and I met, and Pam went her own way. I have not seen her since, much to my regret. But I did learn that she had helped Marianne Faithfull get to grips with her heroin addiction. Marianne has talked about it often, how Pam gave her a place to stay and found her a doctor to give her the right treatment. If you wanted a bed for the night, Pam would be the one I'd turn to.

34

McGOUGH AND McGEAR

Sometime in the summer of 1967 I got a call from Paul. It was around seven in the evening. He said he was at Abbey Road producing a record featuring his brother Mike McGear and Roger McGough. It was a poetry album but there would be plenty of music. He needed a tenor player and asked if I was free. I told him I would be more than happy to join the band and drove to the studio. I parked in the road not far from the now historic Zebra crossing and carried my tenor saxophone into Studio One. Paul was standing by the door and took me in to meet the other musicians.

I knew Roger and Mike from The Scaffold, who were three fine Liverpool poets (the third being John Gorman) already established in the music charts. They were soon to have a number one with 'Lily The Pink'. Paul introduced me to the other musicians who I didn't know at the time. They included Jimi Hendrix, Zoot Money and Dave Mason. Gary Leeds was also there. So was Spencer Davis and Viv Prince. Jane Asher was around, too, to do some screaming on one of the tracks.

The atmosphere was very much workaday. No egos. Roger was older than everyone and adopted a genteel headmaster's approach to the proceedings. Paul was by far the most famous but didn't let it get in the way. He was happy to take a back seat and spend his time organising the parts and chatting with everyone individually about what he wanted them to do. I was to imitate on the tenor what Jane did vocally – scream. That was it. But it had to be the right kind of scream, using the highest notes I could play, so I went into a corner and practised. Oddly enough, a lot of avant-garde players used a screaming sound so I aimed for that. You bite on the reed so the air gets thinned out and the sound is compressed. I still do tenor sax screaming when the tune needs a lift.

Meanwhile, Paul had discovered a large electric keyboard, a sort of prototype of today's sampling machines. It had the sound of every known instrument and could be programmed to play any rhythmic accompaniment you wanted. Paul found a ragtime tempo and a bunch of banjos and suggested it for a section of Roger's early masterpiece, 'Summer With Monika'. Roger had a charming smile. He used it and told Paul that he had imagined the section would be one of the few that had no background sound. And that's what he ended up with.

I worked a lot with Roger over the years. Our two-man readings began when we were invited to perform at a Hay-on-Wye Festival sometime in the early Seventies. Roger read his own work and I read as E. J. Thribb (17). It went down very well and so we decided to get our agents to fix up other festivals and poetry readings. I think we read together for around ten years off and on. Roger's poems are deceptive. On the surface they can sound a little trite, partly because they are so well crafted. People say things like 'I could do that'. The obvious point is that they didn't. It is a rule that the easier something seems, the harder it is to do.

One of my favourite sections of 'Summer With Monika' is 'Ten Milk Bottles'. It is a perfect example of using a light surface to evoke something much deeper.

I would like to think E. J. Thribb's poems had something of Roger's depth but they were not intended to be more than a parody. But every so often the Bard from Balham (where it is thought Eric Jarvis Thribb lives) comes up with a line that reaches out. When the Fifties pop crooner Donald Peers died in 1973, Thribb penned his customary eulogy. On its publication, his widow wrote a very touching letter to the *Eye* thanking Thribb for, as she put it, 'the truly wonderful and moving tribute to my late and most dearly beloved husband, Donald'.

Here is the poem, with a variant of the usual opening line. Not 'So, farewell then'.

In Memoriam
Donald Peers

So, popular singer,
The music has
Faded on the air
Leaving behind
An eerie silence.

Personally I am too
Young to remember
The tunes that
Endeared you to
The hearts of
Millions.

Normally I would ask
Keith's mum
To give me the
Relevant information

But
She is away
With her sister
In Frinton
And will not
Be back
For two weeks.

Roger was always very kind about Thribb. In time we were both asked to be chairmen of the Chelsea Arts Club, Roger being the first non-painter to hold the post. We now meet once a year for the dinner given to the former chairman by the incoming chairman. Roger still has a ponytail, wears an earring and looks like a pop star, which he is in many ways. His smile remains charming. Especially when we talk about the track that might have sounded better with banjos.

35

A BUTCHER'S APRON

I never knew Mary Quant. I might have met her only once on *AWSG*. But I do know that Mary Quant did not invent the mini skirt. Fact. She made it popular. And in a way you could say that they are much the same thing. But not exactly the same. Lots of people in the 1870s were messing about with motorised transport but it was Karl Benz who is now acclaimed as the very first inventor of the motorcar. He took out a patent which proves it. You can't patent a mini skirt. To put matters to right, Mary Quant was just one of many young designers who were experimenting with style to fit the new decade well before the Sixties. But the actual originator of the very first mini skirt, the prototype if you like, was a Royal College art student called Felicity Innes.

Felicity had just married Brian Innes when we met at a Royal College of Arts summer dance. Brian was an art student at the Chelsea College and an enthusiastic jazz drummer. Along with a number of other art students, Brian formed the Temperance Seven, a retro vaudeville band that went on to make a string of hit records. In their early days, the band played at RCA dances. The summer dance was the biggest event of the art student's social calender and students from all over London would queue to get a ticket. Felicity never missed one. She went partly to help Brian carry his old kit of Twenties drums (complete with washboard, wood blocks and cow bells) but mainly to jive. And Felicity was good. She stood out. Her short skirt stood out.

Felicity was in love with the look that the French singer

and actress Juliette Gréco had created. It was unique to Gréco but you can see the origins of her costume and *maquillage* in her role as the female dancer of the French cabaret Apache Dance. Gréco (still living as I write, aged ninety-two) had shoulder-length black hair worn loose over her shoulders and she painted her face white. She wore purple lipstick and made her big eyes even larger with black eyeliner. It was a look Felicity could not hope to imitate. Felicity's natural hair colour was fair and she had cupid lips. They were not wide like Gréco's. Her face was less dominated by cheekbones and she was ten years younger. But there was one aspect of the Gréco look that had nothing to do with genes.

Gréco wore the nearest thing you could get to a mini skirt. Felicity had to have one like it. But you couldn't buy a short skirt, not then, not unless it was the kind ballet dancers wear. Felicity did contemplate a tutu for a while but clearly it was not an option. You couldn't turn up at a jazz night dressed as a *Swan Lake* prima ballerina. But the tutu served as inspiration, and in time the dancer's frilly frock became the mini skirt. The first universal item of female clothing since the fig leaf.

Felicity told me how it happened. She was in a butcher's shop off the Fulham Road buying half a pound of pork sausages and noted that the butcher's waist apron was just the right length for a skirt that you could dance in easily. She asked the butcher if he had an apron to spare. He said he did and put it in Felicity's bag along with the bangers. When she got home Felicity sewed up the sides so it became a cloth tube. Or a very short dress. But there was a problem. Being so short, the hemline exposed a lot of her thighs. And when she danced it revealed more than just her thighs. To preserve her modesty, she bought a pair of matt black ballet tights. At the same time she got some ballet shoes and that was the look that was to dominate the Sixties. Butcher's apron. Flat shoes. Black tights. Big heavily made-up eyes and long slender legs. And it is a look that never went away. And nor has the notion that Mary Quant invented it.

Mary's rise to fame is no secret. She went to Blackheath High School and then did a degree at Goldsmiths College. Her first job was working in Mayfair for a high-class milliner called Erik. By the time she married Alexander Plunket Greene, Mary was designing chic clothes for girls in their late teens and early twenties. Plunket Greene had a pal called Archie McNair who was a lawyer.

At the time Mary met Archie, he was making a lot of money from the Fifties coffee bar fad. He managed skiffle groups and skiffle was big business. One of his groups, the Chas McDevitt Skiffle Group, actually had a number one hit, 'Freight Train'. It sold millions. Archie was born into a family who were members of the Plymouth Brethren. This was not Archie's style. He didn't want austerity and religious extremism. He wanted skiffle and coffee with froth on the top. He had a genuine ability to spot a trend and the Swinging Sixties were about to happen. He could see that young working girls had money to spend on their outfits but the outfits hanging on the rails of high street shops were anything but swinging. All they could buy were full skirts and dull blouses. The Fifties look. The style their mothers wore. Archie, Alex and Mary were quick to supply the need. They cooked up a company called the Ginger Group which sold pretty and inexpensive outfits to teenagers desperate for a change. They opened a shop called Bazaar on the King's Road where they sold all sorts of clothes for young girls. But their big seller was the mini skirt – by a mile.

A close friend of Mary once told me: 'Mary would be the first to say that the idea for a mini skirt came more from a careful observation and study of street fashions at that time. Art students in particular were always coming up with original ideas and art schools themselves were the hothouses of new trends and fashions.'

In the years that followed the advent of the mini skirt, Felicity and I spent a lot of time together in her small flat overlooking Baron's Court underground station. She was anything but bitter about the way Mary had taken all the credit. Just a little sad about the way history gets reported and distorted. 'I know how it happened, even if others don't,' she would say. 'It was in many ways an accident. I just loved Juliette Gréco and did my best to copy her look. And others copied me.'

The King's Road is not a million miles from the Royal College of Art. Perhaps Mary just happened to look out the window of Bazaar one day and see Felicity Innes on her way to a dance and somehow the image stuck.

In later years Felicity moved to live alone in a small cottage in Somerset. It was in a very remote area and she had no phone. She lived frugally, making do as she always had. Resourceful. We wrote to each other often until one morning I got a letter in which she said that she was seriously ill. I wrote back at once. I waited a couple of weeks. I then wrote again but I got no reply.

36

THE JAFFA CAKE MAN

When ITV was given a licence to broadcast and to transmit ads, there was a shortage of know-how when it came to making them. American TV had been showing ads from the very start but there was no history or experience of telly advertising in the UK. There were ads made for the cinema shown between films but these were low-budget affairs. (A still photo showing the interior of the curry house in the High Street.)

What UK advertising agencies did was to make carbon copies of the American ads. Viewers were told in the four-minute commercial breaks in *Take Your Pick* and *Double Your Money* that 'Fairy Snow forces grey out and forces white in', 'Hartley's jam tastes better than home made' and 'One thousand and one cleans a big, big carpet, for less than half the price'. You can see them on YouTube. These ads were all produced on the cheap by agencies with little knowledge and are viewed now with some amusement.

But the Sixties changed the way ads were made. A new generation of ad men created agencies to make the most out of TV advertising. Many of them were from art schools. Ridley Scott Associates was one. In the early Seventies they produced the iconic Hovis ad of a baker's boy pushing a bike load of bread up a hill with an ee-by-gum voice-over and music from Dvorak's *New World* Symphony. The North. Solid. Good sense. A loaf of bread that was value for money. Some cite it as the greatest ad ever. It was actually filmed in Dorset.

The old ponderous style of filming and presentation had given way to slick cutting and a sense of immediacy.

Endorsement was already part of the ad man's bag of tricks, especially in the States where you would regularly find the likes of Ronald Reagan endorsing Chesterfield fags. It was soon to make its mark in the UK and became very big in the Sixties. The public wanted faces they knew selling soap and chocolates. George Best endorsed eating eggs. 'Go to work on an egg' was the catchphrase. Tony Hancock advertised eggs in the summer and the catchphrase was changed to 'Have a holiday on an egg'. Simon Dee promoted crisps. European Song Contest winner Sandie Shaw took off her shoes (her trademark) to sell Lux toilet soap. Fernandel overdid his French accent (his trademark) to introduce the English to Dubonnet. If agencies couldn't pay Julie Christie enough to endorse Wood Nymph shampoo they got an actress who looked like her. Because I had a name at the time and my face would do for the part of any louche-looking pop star I got a lot of work doing ads.

The first one I did was for Martell Cognac. It was for German TV and there was to be a still photo session for magazines and another for the telly. A bright account executive at, I think, Ogilvy & Mather, thought I would look just like Mozart with a wig and dressed in an eighteenth-century outfit. To my surprise, I did look a bit like the Austrian *wunderkind*.

The script went roughly as follows. I would be playing period piano with a buxom lass in a low-cut bodice sitting on my knee. Suddenly I stop playing and pick up a glass of cognac. I raise it to my companion and wink. She smiles and we could all guess what came next. Naughty old Mozart. I ended up having a lot of fun and became a lot richer. And drunk. It was real booze and there were a lot of takes. Nothing pays as well as an ad. The lass on my knee was strikingly beautiful and married to the photographer (Colin) and we all three became good friends after the session. He let me have a sheet of contacts of the session and I used one of the head shots for the inside cover of my first collection of *Private Eye* cartoons.

Advert number two was for Rennies indigestion tablets. I was cast as a pop singer who gets indigestion on stage in the middle of singing his big hit in front of thousands of screaming fans. My face turns from an emotional involvement with the song's sentiment to one painfully expressing stomach cramps. I am not sure there was a great deal of difference. The band backing me was Amen Corner. Their lead singer, Andy Fairweather Low, didn't take part as I was supposed to be him. Instead, Andy sat in the back row and sulked throughout the shooting, in spite of my spirited efforts between takes to give him advice.

I had seen a lot of showbiz movies about making good so I knew the lines. I told him that he had to be a pro, accept the rough with the smooth, and that showbiz broke a lot of hearts and you had to be real tough to make it to the top, kid. He took no notice. I think it made him worse. As it worked out, Andy did make it to the top. Or pretty close. The Rennies ad was shot by Bob Godfrey. He was a good pal and Nick Park has often said how much Bob's work influenced him. I would say Bob influenced everyone. He was in his nineties when he died in 2013, having won every award an animator can get.

The biggest ad I did was for McVitie's Jaffa Cakes, named after Jaffa oranges. It went nationwide, which meant it was seen by an average of twenty million viewers a day in 1967. Not all ads go nationwide. Half are regional. Local ads for local products. For about a year I was the Jaffa Cake Man.

Strangers would stop me in the street and tell me how much they enjoyed their Jaffa Cakes. I once signed an unopened packet – 'To Aunty Pat, best wishes, the Jaffa Cake Man'.

The shoot took two days. My role was one of a driver in a bank robbers' getaway car. But I am so busy eating my Jaffa Cake that I forget where I am and my gang gets nabbed. I earned a thousand a day plus royalties and a healthy aversion to cheap biscuits.

37

MY GENERATION

Pete Townshend was the featured guest on the first edition of *AWSG*. We made a film of The Who's working life, and after it was shown I interviewed Pete along with members of the audience, who asked questions. Pete was both articulate and informative about the band's musical philosophy and attitude towards the way the press had overstated the personal differences that existed within the band. He said it was inevitable that in small bands there would be times of tension and he was equally frank about their use of drugs. Not a common admission at the time. Even having a wife was kept quiet, as was the case with Cynthia and John. Agents liked their stars free of a personal life. The image they preferred was of the rock star as hero, not someone who helps with the dishes and changes the baby's nappies. Even the Sixties revolution did not allow fans to see rock heroes as human.

When I knew him on a day-to-day basis Pete was prone to losing his self-control. This frequently expressed itself through smashing up his guitar on stage. Mick strutted as if he was suffering from an epileptic fit. The diminutive Freddie of the Dreamers jumped off stage (often twice his height) and then jumped back on. Tom Jones battled with a barrage of ladies' underwear. Pete smashed his guitar. It wasn't a gimmick. I sensed a genuine underlying anger there. There was a time early on in our friendship when we agreed we should try to write songs together. In 1966 Pete lived in Chelsea. His flat was at the river end of Old Church Street and, not needing the extra bedroom, he turned it into a recording studio. I once went there with a song called 'Sitting On The Fence'. Pete tried putting down a backing riff but the very expensive tape deck was not responding in the way he wanted. He tried half a dozen times to record the track but nothing happened. Instead of simply calling the supplier and asking for an explanation, Pete yanked the tape deck from the desk and hurled it across the studio. He then dug out the reel and tore the tape to shreds. With the session and tape machine in ruins, Pete said there was a good pub down the street and we should go there and forget about writing songs for the day.

Sometimes we would eat together with Keith Moon and John Entwistle at the Bistro Vino because it was open late. Pete was not fussy about food and Keith was mainly interested in getting stoned. John was easygoing. Food or dope. He was easily pleased and was a better than average rock bass player. Roger never joined us. As I discovered later, Pete and Roger didn't have a lot in common. Pete's father had been a musician and Pete came from an arts background. Roger was bright but not original. Not in the way that Pete was. And his fuse was even shorter. He once punched Pete in the mouth in the middle of a gig and got himself chucked out of the band for a while. I can't say I warmed to Roger but his aggressive nature fitted the image of The Who and the songs Pete wrote for his band.

Pete was fond of American cars when I hung out with him. He said once that he had always fancied owning a Cadillac. One Saturday in the summer of 1966 my phone rang. It was Pete. He had just got a royalty cheque for 'My Generation'. He'd seen a Cadillac convertible for sale in Balham and wanted me to go with him and look it over. Later in the day we saw the car – ivory white with burgundy leather upholstery and not a speck of rust. High mileage but showroom condition. It was all Pete wanted.

We rode around in it together for a while, then Pete said he had a gig in Brighton that night and would drive to the venue in his new car. We didn't see each other for a couple of months. When we met up I asked about the Cadillac and he told me he'd crashed it into a tree on the way to Brighton that night because the left-hand drive was hard to handle. I asked Pete if he had been injured and Pete said he was fine but the car was a write-off. The front was all smashed up and the wheels had come off. I asked where it was and Pete said it was probably still in front of the tree he'd driven into. He added that he was driving a white Transit van he'd picked up for twenty quid until the next royalty cheque came in.

You can see the very first edition of *AWSG* with The Who on YouTube, plus a few others. You can't see them all because the BBC wiped them so they could reuse the tapes.

38

STRIPPING OFF

Terry Knight studied painting and illustration at Camberwell School of Arts and Crafts. Before Camberwell he went to Archbishop Temple's School where I was a pupil. He was a little older than me so I never knew him there. I met Terry when he opened Gear, the first shop anywhere to sell stripped pine furniture and merchandise that harked back to a period without plastic or Formica. It became the blueprint for a million shops that have opened since, selling copies of what Gear sold in their original form – genuine enamel road signs, genuine period pine tables, genuine period rocking chairs, genuine period everything.

Although Terry had complete control over the merchandise, he had no head for money. Tom Salter, a conventionally dressed and prematurely balding man with a thick brown moustache, supplied the money. When Terry left art school he couldn't get anywhere selling pictures so he went into the film industry where he built sets and learned about lighting and design. Because of this, he got to know where to find furniture and props. Hollywood has vast buildings where they store large props. Not Pinewood. Not in the Fifties and early Sixties. Film companies hired specialists to find props, especially for period movies.

Terry knew where to look. He picked up pine tables and chairs, old enamel signs, old kitchen cupboards and pine doors, and benches and desks. He stripped the pine furniture used for film sets, cleaned up the enamel posters and sold them to a whole new generation unhappy with G Plan and traditional decor. Tom came up with the deposit for a lease on a Carnaby Street shop.

Gear was not an immediate success. It took a while for the concept to catch on but once a few pop names and film people let it be known they were getting their interiors from Gear, things snowballed. Everyone wanted an old Esso Petrol sign to hang on their Dulux-white wall and a freshly stripped door leading to a kitchen full of Union Jack mugs. It was as essential as a record collection full of Stones and Beatles albums and a wardrobe full of mini skirts and John Stephen jackets.

Gear made Carnaby Street, with a little help from John Stephen's clothing empire at the opposite end of the cut-through from Great Marlborough Street to Beak Street. But there was a problem. Before long the supply of old kitchen tables and Victorian doors more or less dried up. The number of original Edwardian tables and chairs that can survive a century and two world wars is finite. The solution was simple, though. Make the new stuff look like old stuff. Enamel posters were the first items to get the treatment. They were cheap and easy to produce, and Gear sold millions. Tables and chairs were more of a problem. Terry got some carpenters from the film studios to make stripped-pine copies and within a few years the demand was so great that Tom and Terry gave up on furniture and settled for selling printed Union Jacks on everything from teacloths to cushions.

In the middle of Carnaby Street at that time was a vegetarian restaurant called Cranks. It was next to Vince Green's kiosk-sized boutique that specialised in young single men's underwear. Cranks opened about the same time as Gear. It sold vegetable soup, brown rice risotto and wholemeal lasagna. The salads had lots of beans in them and the wholemeal bread was homemade. The owners, David, Kay and Daphne, were early pioneers of recycling. What they couldn't sell fresh at lunchtime they heated up for dinner. And what was still unsold was turned into a stew for the next day's lunch. And the stew they didn't sell at lunchtime went back on the supper menu. Cranks made millions before going out of business. Let's face it, there are only so many times you can reheat a whole-grain lentil bake.

While Gear was in its early stages Terry asked me to supply him with paintings and monotypes. I did a lot of monotypes of Cassius Clay, as he was known then, and scenes from the American Civil War copied from the many photos taken between 1861 and 1865. I also did monotypes of publicity shots from early black-and-white movies. Not many artists do them. It usually entails a lot of work but the price you can ask will never reflect it. An edition can make a fat profit if you sell the whole print run. Picasso did them now and again. Terry saw these images as an ideal pictorial complement to the furniture and fittings. And he was right. The monotypes became bestsellers and a number of less well established artists copied them. Terry once told me that Michael English, who was to become extremely successful during the late Sixties and early Seventies, came into the shop as an unknown with a portfolio of his work and said that he 'could do a Fantoni' for half the price. Terry politely refused the offer.

I got to know Michael. I liked his work. He was very gifted and he had the knack of working in any style he chose, latching on to the latest trend. He painted the way some people play the piano. They hear a tune once and they can play it straight off. Note perfect. Michael did some quite wonderful posters towards the end of the Sixties for his pal Nigel Waymouth. (Not to be confused with Alexander George Thynn, 7th Marquess of Bath, styled Viscount Weymouth.) Nigel opened a shop on the King's Road called Granny Takes a Trip. Michael used an airbrush at the time and his hyper-realistic images became an instant hit. Michael died in 2009. Nigel is still going strong. But not Terry.

Terry got arrested for something one evening and was sent to jail where he suddenly died. I tried to find out why and how. I found the prison but no one I spoke to there would tell me anything. The last time I saw Tom he wouldn't discuss how Terry died and when you look for Terry Knight's name in connection with Gear, it is nowhere to be seen. The only Terry Knight you will find on the web is the dead rock and roll singer. The Terry Knight I knew was not forty when he died in police custody.

39

NOT SWINGING BUT REVOLVING

There was a ring on the bell at 60 South Side late one Sunday evening in early 1966. Not a lot happened on Sunday evenings so I always kept them free for illustrating. I could be sure of getting a good start without any interruptions. The doorbell ringing surprised me. I dipped my brush into the water jar, wiped it clean and answered the door. It was Karl Dallas.

Karl said he was sorry he hadn't let me know he was coming but he was passing and saw my light on and thought he would take the opportunity to pop in. He had an idea he wanted to talk to me about. I invited him in. If Karl had an idea to talk over it was bound to be worth listening to. He was fascinated by social change. He said he'd read endless articles in papers and magazines but no one had published a full account of what it meant to be living in Swinging London. There was no comprehensive guide. Trends and fashions changed overnight but there was a solid core of places that would stand up to the more lasting format of a book. If we produced it quickly and inexpensively it might even sell a lot of copies. I made him a cup of tea, his preferred tipple, and poured myself a brandy, which is mine.

Karl went on to say that he wanted me to design and illustrate the book and my name should take the major credit. The book would be called *Swinging London: A Guide to Where the Action Is – Illustrated by Barry Fantoni*. Karl would do the research and write the copy. He said it wouldn't take long because all the listings were easy to access. The only problem was that Karl didn't have any money. He had just enough to pay for a print run of a thousand copies but there was nothing in the bank for my fee. But he was sure the book would sell. With my name on the cover (which I eventually hand-lettered to save costs), we would sell millions and by the end of the year we would make a fortune. We could share it. Half and half. A half million each. It was the way Karl worked. Enthusiasm first, nothing second. I agreed.

The book was published and criticised by some reviewers for being ephemeral. In my experience the vast majority of reviewers are uncomfortable when not reviewing books written by their Oxbridge chums. In this case the snobby elite failed to note that the book was a *guide*. Where to go and what to do. It said so in big red letters on the cover and was stated a dozen and more times in the text. In spite of the poor reviews, the book sold out. But we didn't reprint. No guidebook has a long shelf life. Not even the one written by Karl Baedeker.

I had fun working with Karl. He was a man who relished the chance to share his likes as well his dislikes. There wasn't much he disapproved of but he didn't think much of Bob Dylan. This was unusual. Everyone else saw Dylan as the big cheese. Karl once told me: 'Dylan is a fraud who made his name on the pretence that he hung out with all the great folk singers and learned his "trade" from them. Bollocks. Dylan went to Woody's house a couple of times and built his whole career on how well he knew him.'

As well as being extremely well informed, Karl was a man who spoke his mind.

He became a committed Christian for the last years of his life and we always kept in touch. He died in 2016. Some you miss more than others. I miss Karl. He never lost his thirst for new experiences or his belief that there was a right way to live and a wrong way.

If you want a copy of *Swinging London* you will find one on the web and it will cost you forty quid. In my introduction you will read this.

> Fleet Street hacks when hung up for two thousand words take a taxi into Carnaby Street or King's Road and write a fab load of switched-on rubbish that gets subbed down to a caption for a photo of some swinging dolly with her skirt up over her knickers. London has been swinging for ages, it's just that *Time* magazine and supplements hadn't noticed it.

I haven't changed my view. Just tarted it up a bit.

In 1966 I won a *Melody Maker* award. The actual object is made of black onyx with a modern-style silver saxophone player in the middle and the name of the winner in silver underneath. It is free-standing like a photo frame and you can put it on your desk, a bookshelf in your room or a bedside table. I gave mine to my mum and she put it on top of her telly.

I was presented with the award at a reception held in the top-floor restaurant of the recently opened Post Office Tower. One month after Postmaster General Tony Benn and holiday-camp tycoon Billy Butlin jointly cut the ribbon, *Melody Maker* decided it would be an ideal venue for their annual award ceremony. The restaurant, as well as everything else in the tower, was seen as a giant leap forward in technology, an emblem of the Sixties – not swinging but revolving. Benn called it 'the white heat of technology'. You could eat your

Chicken in a Basket looking towards Stepney at nine at night and then your Black Forest Gateau an hour later, looking towards Neasden.

As an award winner I had been invited along with around a hundred or so fellow awardees, pop stars, pop journalists, pop stars' mums, dads, nans, aunts and uncles and groupies. There were always plenty of groupies and hangers-on. After lunch was declared over and the tables and chairs cleared away, the paper's editor, Jack Hutton, climbed onto the makeshift podium and reminded everybody that the winners of all the sections, such as Top Female Vocalist and Top Jazz Drummer, were voted for by readers, not what he called 'a bribed jury like all the other polls'.

Jack got a big cheer because everyone felt better about being voted for by readers and not hacks, and more drinks were handed out. He then announced that due to a cock-up in the awards department all we would be taking home with us was a framed certificate, signed by him, because the actual awards had not been made in time. There was less cheering to this announcement. None. Pop stars like their onyx and silver.

I was standing next to Paul, who, with Ringo, was there to collect awards for Top Group, Top Songwriters and Top International Group on behalf of the other two Beatles. It was all taking a lot of time to get organised and it wasn't made any easier by the fact that the restaurant was gently spinning. Not fast but spinning nonetheless.

By the time all the speeches were over, all the guests and recipients were on one side and the *Melody Maker* team with the awards were on the other. We were divided by the central concrete support pillar and the piles of chairs and tables that were not being used. Because no one knew how to stop the restaurant moving, the only option was for the winners to climb over the furniture. Everyone did their best. Johnny Dankworth – Top Alto Sax – got stuck and needed a couple of wine waiters to help him. Dusty was also offered a hand but responded by throwing a pile of cream buns at anyone who came near. By the time I went up to get my award for Top Male TV Celebrity I was looking out at Neasden and Jack Hutton had the view of Tower Bridge.

When Jack retired, his job was taken by Ray Coleman, a very fine writer and just the right man to see the *Melody Maker* through the rest of the Sixties, a period when it became the most influential UK music paper of all time. We became good pals and would often have supper together at his house in Shepperton. Ray wrote over a dozen biographies, including those of Dusty, Phil Collins, Frank Sinatra, John Lennon, Macca, Brian Epstein, Eric Clapton and Rod Stewart. He once told me that, while writing his two-volume biography of Lennon, he was sitting in the back of John's Rolls, making notes. The Beatles had been filming on location, and thousands of fans had turned up. As the Rolls edged its way through the screaming mob, a female fan scratched her name on the paintwork. Ray was horrified. 'Did you see that?' he asked John, who replied: 'They paid for it, they can do what they like.'

The *Melody Maker* award meant a lot to me. I might not have had a jot of talent but that was not the issue. I was popular with the readers. If you wanted someone to open a supermarket in Romford or Moss Side, the organisers could hire me to do the job, and because I was popular, count on a good turnout. I opened a lot of supermarkets. I would give a short speech about the fish fingers on offer, snip the red silk, have a snap taken with the manager and put a grand in cash in my pocket. A lot more than the BBC paid me for introducing a half-hour pop show live on TV and viewed by sixteen million people. There was no Chris Evans in my day.

When my mum moved into sheltered housing six months before she died the *MM* Award was the only item she took with her. The award was a sign that her working-class East End origins were no barrier to her boy making something of himself. When she died I took it back. It represents her faith in me.

Melody Maker folded in 2000. By then it had become just another pop rag.

Benn shut the Post Office Tower off from diners in the Seventies after the IRA said they intended to blow it up. He smoked a pipe and drank tea from a mug and had wide staring eyes. The *Eye* called him Loony Benn.

40

FREDDY

I met Freddy when she had just turned seventeen. If she had another name I never heard her mention it. That was it. Freddy had left home for fun in Swinging London. She was one of many. She had applied for a job at the *Eye* but had no experience of anything to do with magazines. Or anything else. She arrived for the interview in a black dress and black hat and a silver crucifix on a chain around her neck. It was clear that making tea was not her thing. Freddy's interview lasted about five minutes. There was a glass window in the office and I watched as she crossed her legs in a short skirt, lit a cigarette and used her seductive smile to get herself hired. But it didn't work. The *Eye* needed qualified tea makers.

Freddy didn't get the job and told me on her way out that she lived on and off with a boyfriend in Fulham. He was in the animated-film business and about my age. Freddy said she would like to see me again and I told her to come to 60 South Side. I told her I would like to paint her. I loved her outfit and her body wasn't bad, either.

She came the next day at noon. She was wearing the same outfit she had worn the previous day. The first thing she said was that she had been up all night and needed to sleep for an hour. She then got undressed and climbed into my bed. While Freddy took her nap I set up the studio for painting a portrait and pottered around, quietly squeezing out black paint and cleaning my brushes until she was ready. When she got up, Freddy came into the studio naked. I have seldom seen a more beautiful naked body. Freddy had dark copper hair, and she painted her full lips more or less the same colour. Her skin was flawless, pale as white marble, and there was no colour in her cheeks. Her eyes were washed-out emerald. Like the sea-worn glass you find on beaches.

It struck me that I should paint Freddy nude first. The pure white of her skin against the deep red of her hair. The large silver cross dangling between her breasts. These contrasting elements seemed to me at the time to symbolise much of what the Sixties had become – a contrast of the old and the new. Or something. I might have been drinking the night before. In any event I decided to stick to my original plan and paint Freddy in her black outfit. I asked her to get dressed.

Freddy took no time getting ready and came back into the studio. She made herself comfortable on the model's chair facing me. I told her to keep as still as possible and started to rough in where her head and shoulders would be on the canvas with a faint ochre line. It was part of a technique I had learned at Camberwell Art School. Some artists use charcoal to rough in basic shapes. Cézanne used cobalt blue and you can see it in all his later paintings.

As I worked, Freddy told me that she had been born in Malta and her father was in the army. She had no home and lived with various boyfriends. Like the one in Fulham. She said they all shared the same casual attitude to sex and relationships. Sometimes she would share a bed with a girlfriend. She told me all this in the first few minutes and said almost nothing else until the session was over. When I said I had done all I could for the day, Freddy rolled a joint with some grass the boyfriend in Fulham had given her and I poured myself a glass of brandy and made coffee. Then we both took stock of what I had painted.

Her body outline and some features were in place. And her large black brimmed hat was half finished. The black background was there and so was the place where her silver cross would hang. Dead centre. I told her it would take half a dozen sittings to complete the portrait, although I would work on it from photos that I would take the next time. Freddy said that was fine and we made a date for the second sitting. It was to be a week away. But Freddy didn't show.

A few days later, she met a guy who was making a film about the Rolling Stones at a party her film-maker boyfriend had been invited to. In the course of the evening Freddy found herself in bed with the man who carted Charlie Watts' drums off and on the band bus. It was the key to the door of the Stones' inner circle. All groups had them. Most were pretty wild in the early days, and as far as I knew, the Stones' was the wildest by far.

Even though Freddy didn't come back to South Side to have her portrait completed, she did drop by to tell me news of how her life was shaping up. Her one-night-stand with the roadie had led her to becoming intimate with other members of the Stones' entourage. There were times I would go with Freddy to hang out with her new friends but I never really got on with Mick and Keith. They never had much to say. Unlike Paul and John, Ray, Jimmy and Pete, who all came from a fine arts background, and had broad interests outside rock and roll, a conversation with a Rolling Stone didn't get much beyond basics. 'All right?' 'Yeah.'

Keith had studied art in Sydenham but didn't seem to have learned much. By his own admission, all he did was try to copy Chuck Berry licks while the rest of the class were grappling with the complexities of the Golden Section and how to stretch a canvas. As far as I can recall, Keith never talked about anything to do with painting. Charlie was OK. He'd done some graphic art and was a jazz drummer at heart. As to the others: Mick was and is an LSE student. He talked about cricket when the mood took him. And money. Mick was keen on anything to do with money. Brian was out of it most of the time and had nothing to say about anything. Bill was usually shagging someone somewhere else.

But you could talk to Charlie about Buddy Rich and Gene Krupa. He knew about album cover design, and, if you mentioned the great jazz album cover designer David Stone Martin, Charlie wasn't fazed. He'd tell you the cover he liked best. (All of them.) I had a soft spot for Charlie because he knew that as good a drummer as he was, he was a long way behind the drummers he admired, and I know that he worked hard to improve. And he did. He was generous with his time and money, and at one time formed a big band simply to give out-of-work jazz musicians a job.

In the end I stopped hanging out with Freddy and her new pals. Then I lost touch with her altogether, until recently. I got an email, sent via the *Eye*, saying she had moved to San Francisco. She was living as happily as ever in someone else's bed, enjoying the occasional smoke and wondering what had become of her portrait.

41

DUD AND DAVE

For a long time into their partnership, Dud was very much the '. . . and Dud' member of the duo. By 1968 he was fed up with being thought of as the 'other half' and decided to promote himself as a solo performer. He formed a company with John Wells and director Joe McGrath to make a movie. Joe had just finished filming parts of *Casino Royale* with Peter Sellers and was looking for someone with Peter's talents to work with. Dudley had them all and some to spare.

Joe and I had met when he did some voices on a floppy disc the *Eye* produced in the Sixties. These were 45s on flimsy vinyl that were stuck to the cover and given away free. Joe lived near to where Peter was living at the time and they were pals. Joe bought one of my monotypes, 'Broadway Melody of 1936', for Peter's fortieth birthday. He also gave him a copy of my detective novel *Mike Dime*, which was in the style of Raymond Chandler. It was Joe who found Peter dead. He had got a call from Peter earlier in the evening saying that he wasn't feeling too well, and could Joe maybe drop by when he had a moment free. Joe went at once and there was no answer when he rang the bell. As it happens, Joe had a key and let himself in. He found Peter in bed, dead.

When Joe told me this story some time later he said that my book was on his bedside table. Joe said it was the last book Peter read. When we did a reprint I suggested we put a new quote on the cover: 'I died laughing' Peter Sellers. The publishers didn't think it was a good idea.

30 Is a Dangerous Age, Cynthia! is the film that Joe, John and Dudley knocked up. A light comedy that gave a lot of time to showing how sexy Dudley looked when not dressed in a cloth cap, plastic mac and doing his best not to corpse at Cook's endless improvisations. And the writing trio made sure all their acting mates were given a part. Some big, some small. Dudley played a character called Rupert Street (no, it wasn't funny then, either). I played an art-gallery owner and David Hemmings played a painter pal of Rupert. Or maybe it was the other way round. But it doesn't matter because they cut the scene. David had made *Blow-Up* a year before and the film had already been released to great acclaim. *Blow-Up* is now considered by those who know as one of the worst films ever made but it was a massive hit at the time. Clearly it was not possible to show David, who was now an international star, playing a small cameo role in a light-hearted movie starring Dudley Moore.

Dudley's first wife, Suzy Kendall, was in the movie, although she wasn't married to him when we started shooting. Suzy was a natural blonde with slightly too thin legs and a slightly too wide smile to be thought of as another Marilyn Monroe, as all blondes hoped to be at that time. And her upper body left a lot to the imagination. So not another Mamie Van Doren either, who *was* another Marilyn Monroe. We spent time talking during breaks in filming. Her conversation was largely along the lines of 'Can I trust him?' I could find nothing helpful to reassure her. Dudley was an organ scholar. A great jazz pianist. A wit. As bright as they come. He was easily attracted to women and women were easily attracted to Dudley. When pressed for a response, I said something like 'Take heed, love. Leopards don't change their spots.' But she married him anyway.

After the movie was shot David Hemmings and I became good pals. I got him into the Chelsea Arts Club – I had been a member since 1964 – and we spent a lot of time playing snooker or drinking white wine in the leafy garden when the summer came. David always picked up the bill, no matter how many members joined us at the table. I have seldom met a man so happy to see other people having fun, or so willing to foot the bill.

Much later, in 2003, David asked my band to play at his son's wedding. I am including this tale, even though it is not strictly Sixties, because it says a lot about the David I knew. The reception was on an island on the Thames. You had to get there on a little boat. A very little boat. It only just held the musicians and their instruments. As we landed David passed out bottles of Champagne and said there was plenty more. Then the bride and groom arrived on a riverboat decked out with white roses.

I had never met David's son, Nolan, until the wedding. I was taken by just how much he resembled his father. It was as if I was looking at David the day I'd met him on the film set of *30* . . . some forty years back. All through the evening I kept looking at Nolan, fascinated by the similarity. Not only his handsome features but his manners. Open and generous. As for the wedding, it was a lot of fun. It gave me the chance to meet up with a lot of faces I had not seen in while. The reception went on into the early morning. David paid us a fee, although we would have been happy to have done the gig for free.

Two weeks later David died suddenly from a heart attack while filming in Romania. Nothing had suggested that David was in poor health at the reception, and from what I have gathered since, there were no alarm bells to indicate his heart was in bad shape. At the wedding we agreed that we should see more of each other and had fixed up a lunch at the Chelsea Arts Club for later that month. When I heard the news I found it very difficult to believe. No one was more fun to be with on a good night. He was the best company a pal could have. I hope someone will say the same about Nolan.

42

TIME FOR SOME TM

When Paul bought his house at the back of Lord's cricket ground, he was still on the road most of the time. He hardly slept there. He told me more than once that he wanted time off from the endless touring to do other things. He wanted to paint, to experiment with art forms, to make a movie. Paul had been in two Beatles movies directed by Dick Lester, and the idea of directing had crossed his mind. Paul was always trying out new ideas and when he found something that took his interest he did his utmost to master it. It was the same when he discovered Transcendental Meditation (TM).

I was with Paul one afternoon in the late August of 1967 when the phone rang. It was John. He said that he had been given some tickets to a talk on TM by the Maharishi Mahesh Yogi. Paul asked me if I wanted to come as there were some spare tickets. I said I was already following the teachings of Jiddu Krishnamurti – who many believed to be the reincarnation of Krishna – and added that one guru was enough for any man.

Krishnamurti could not have been more different from the Maharishi Mahesh Yogi. The latter was a man in white robes with a long beard who handed out nuggets of inner peace as if they were samples of a new washing powder outside a supermarket. Yet he swayed Paul and the others for over a year and his followers paid him handsomely for his wisdom.

By contrast the incarnation of Krishna was clean shaven, small and slender. Not much taller than a jockey. He had an actor's good looks and when I met him he was wearing a hand-tailored suit, fine silk socks and hand-made Italian shoes. It was at a talk he gave in the main room of Wimbledon Public Library five years before the Maharishi Mahesh Yogi came on the scene.

Krishnamurti only gave his talks at dawn. At six on the dot, as the pale spring sun rose above the grey-slated rooftops of SW19, he entered quietly and sat on a plain wooden chair in the centre of the room. It was packed. There was not an empty seat anywhere. People had come from all over the world because his public appearances were famously rare. His followers could be counted in many thousands. Krishnamurti was quite old in 1963 and restricted his talk to an hour exactly. He then offered his audience a Q&A for thirty minutes. He spoke very quietly and without any affectation. You had to pay attention or you'd miss it.

One thing he said that morning took root in me. He said it often and it is often quoted: 'Religion is the frozen thought of man out of which they build temples.' At this point, an American, who was clearly practised in some kind of formal western religion asked, 'Master, are you laughing at me?' It was clear from his tone and question that he had been to many of Krishnamurti's talks. I later learned he was a retired general who did, in fact, follow Krishnamurti everywhere. There was a short silence. The reply came with a smile. 'No, sir. I am laughing at all of us.' And we all laughed at ourselves.

I should emphasise here that Jiddu Krishnamurti and the Hare Krishna cult are in no way connected, although from the name it might appear so. The bedraggled band that wander around Soho banging drums and chanting are devotees of Abhay Charanaravinda Bhaktivedanta Swami Prabhupada.

I spoke to Paul on the day after he had seen Maharishi

Mahesh Yogi and it was obvious he had been seriously affected. He talked about it in great detail – of exotic ashrams and shaded courtyards full of banyan trees and monkeys running wild in the foothills of the snow-capped Himalayas. It was a world away from a childhood spent on Merseyside. From Penny Lane and Strawberry Fields. Paul was hooked, and so it transpired were John and George. Ringo tagged along as he always did.

In time it became clear that the Maharishi Mahesh Yogi was not all he seemed. He never explained how he had attained the exalted title of 'Maharishi', meaning 'great seer'. Nor did he keep accounts of his financial dealings or pay his taxes. No matter that he demanded expensive gifts (usually Rolls-Royces) and large sums of money (millions), he won people over. The Beatles, film stars from Hollywood and supermodels from Chelsea all flocked to India like '49ers in the Gold Rush. What they saw on offer was a means to obtain the patina of great wisdom. By sitting in the Lotus position for a few hours a day in a state of Transcendental Meditation they would rise above the pampering and adulation that had become their way of life and find the true meaning of whatever it was life was meant to be. In reality, all they did was learn a few of the phoney yogi's bromides. This is one of them: 'Problems are all in your head.'

By the end of the summer of 1967, the cultural revolution took another turn. Mainly in the way people dressed and groomed themselves, which was more than a little connected to the fact that the Beatles and hangers-on had become spiritually enlightened. Blokes now grew droopy moustaches and both sexes wore flowers in their hair. What became dubbed 'Flower Power' took the Sixties generation out of the

King's Road and Carnaby Street and put it in San Francisco, to Haight-Ashbury where old hippies from the Fifties beat years had holed up. The message was now 'peace and love'. Not 'fab and gear'. The Sixties was officially over.

The Flower Power craze, with its imagery drawn from psychedelic experiences, proved to be a boon to illustrators. Bands were desperate to be seen in beads and flowers, and the visual vocabulary changed along with everything else. Pop Art used fonts based on old wood type, hard-edged and often with a shadow. Peter Blake was famous for his shadow fonts. Flower Power was freehand. Loose. Soft. You only have to compare the black-and-white starkness of the cover of *With The Beatles* (1963) to the *Magical Mystery Tour* (1967) to get the picture. The rapid rise in sales of record albums meant plenty of work for those happy enough to fill a twelve-inch square with LSD-inspired wavy lines and bright colours. I was not one of them.

43

AS GOOD AS DAUMIER

Although David Frost presented *TW3*, there were many others responsible for the show being compulsive viewing. I would often hear people talk about the cartoonist who drew as he talked and seemed to make up jokes as he went along. The cartoonist was Timothy Birdsall. And they were right. Tim performed without a script, preferring to let his ideas flow in the way that jazz musicians ad-lib. He'd pick a subject and freeform. And the flow was never routine. Never stale. It was sharp and informative as well as being hugely entertaining. Some cartoonists never get beyond the two-men-on-a-desert-island joke. Tim never even bothered going there. His style was based on the work of Hogarth and Gillray. One critic said that Tim was as good as Daumier.

Tim went to Cambridge, where he met Cook and Booker. He was a year older than both. They had all worked together on *Granta*, the school mag. It is commonly thought that Cook was the key figure in the early days of satire. That is true but only half the story. Tim certainly picked up a lot of Cook's thinking but he gave as much as he got. There are those who say Cook's jokes became more political after meeting Tim. Left to his own, Cook was more fanciful than political. Tim's humour was pretty well only political. His targets were politicians. Tim could never have produced a character like Cook's E. L. Wisty. Cook's attacks on Harold Macmillan were off-beat, such as when he portrayed him in *Beyond the Fringe* as a bumbling old Tory who offered this as advice on surviving a nuclear attack: 'We shall receive four minutes' warning of any impending nuclear attack. Now, some people said, "Oh my goodness me, four minutes, that's not a very long time." But I remind those doubters that some people in this great country of ours can run a mile in four minutes.'

Tim was a heavyweight with a solid right hand and would smack Mac on the chin. Had Daumier been around in 1963, he would have had his work cut out doing a better job of making Macmillan look more grotesque.

When Tim left Cambridge he got a job doing a pocket cartoon for *The Sunday Times* and married a beautiful actress called Jocelyn Britton. Jocelyn was in the 1961 movie *So Evil, So Young*. It was a rip-off of an American film called *So Bad, So Young* and was panned by everyone. But Tim's wife didn't let the reviews bother her. She was a good actress and was devoted to Tim and their small child. When the *Eye* began publishing in October 1961, then-editor Christopher Booker asked him to recreate the effective partnership they had had working on *Granta*. Together they created a series of middle-page spreads that rank alongside the finest satire produced at that, or any other, time. One memorable spread showed leading politicians and public figures milling around Trafalgar Square dressed in fab gear and acting hip. Tim called his cartoon 'Britain gets wyth itte, 1963'.

As well as editing the *Eye*, Booker was also writing with Frost on *TW3*. Being part of the old Cambridge *Granta* team, Tim had a spot on the show. It was where I met him. Backstage one Saturday after transmission. I had drawn an animated cartoon based on a Pop painting that producer Ned Sherrin had seen at my one-man show earlier in the year. *TW3* went out live and it was the first time they had used an animated cartoon. I was asked to be in the studio in case anything went wrong. It didn't, and I did a lot more for the show.

In the week that followed I met Tim again at the *Eye*. We talked for a while and had a drink in the Coach and Horses and discussed cartoons and cartoonists. He knew a lot about the history of political cartooning and said that his ambition was to draw in the traditions of past masters. Large and complex. A full page packed with detail and captions all over the shop. Which is what he did. His style was fluid and, if there was a fault, the words were sometimes a little too dense for the bubbles. Hard to read at a glance. But Tim was a free spirit. His thoughts and actions were often one and the same. The next time we met was in the hospital where he was to die shortly after.

Tim developed leukemia some time in late 1962. It was pernicious and there was no cure. He said plainly that he did not think he would get better and there would be a job going on *TW3* if I wanted it. I said the usual things about not giving up and you never know what they might come with. But we both knew the words meant nothing. In the end I didn't take Tim's job. It wasn't offered, and even if it had been I wasn't the right cartoonist for it. No one was. Instead I illustrated the *TW3* annual that came out later the same year. It was more my style. Black-and-white illustrations. Painted slowly and carefully. Not drawn in a flash of inspiration.

Tim died on 10 June 1963. He was twenty-seven. His contribution to the Sixties revolution, in particular the way cartoons are drawn, largely died with him. He was not around long enough for his name to take hold in the way Scarfe's did. Or Steadman. Others, including me, were to be his heirs and forever grateful.

44

AIRBRUSHED IN

Until the Sixties, publishing in Britain had been a traditional business. Fathers and sons. Old Etonians. Oxbridge. There were few new publishers. The thoroughly decent Paul Hamlyn, with his Octopus Press, was one. Robert Maxwell's Pergamon Press was another. But the majority were still run by men with old money. Collins, who publish the King James Bible, was typical. Out of date and backward-looking. Macmillan was another publishing house with a long history that had not kept up with the times. The same was true of Penguin Books. But it was not their authors who were out of touch. Nor was it the subject matter, which tends to change very little. Crime. Romance. Cooking. Travel. It was a matter of appearance. The presentation. The look. In other words, the cover. It has been said time and again that you can't judge a book by its cover. But it is equally the case that you can't sell a book if the cover is a duffer.

Penguin were the first house anywhere in the world to publish paperback books. It was founder Allen Lane's idea. A book you could carry in your pocket and read on a train between Exeter and London. Lane had just been to see Agatha Christie, a Penguin author who lived in the West Country, when the idea came to him. On the station with only a newspaper to read. 'I'll be on the sports pages in half an hour. But what if I had a lightweight book in my pocket? No heavy cardboard covers. A paper back!'

The first Penguins appeared in 1935 as an imprint of The Bodley Head (founded in 1887). But by the mid-Sixties they had lost their mojo. An American called Peter Mayer took over the running of Lane's company. His brash and arrogant manner, along with his crude knowledge of books, made him extremely unpopular with many. But it didn't bother him. He sacked the old head of design and replaced him with a man called Alan Aldridge. His brief was to revamp their titles from front to back and make them appeal to a mass market of dolly birds and Mods. The choice looked like a winner. Alan was a a trend-setting illustrator who worked with an airbrush and he was given a free hand to do whatever it took to make a jacket look fab.

Alan had very long blonde hair. His considerable reputation had been made by illustrating the Beatles songs which sold in millions. His method of working was to draw a rough outline and get students to airbrush in the colours. The result was that virtually all the books looked like versions of *The Illustrated Beatles Songbook*. Under Alan's supervision, teams of art students spent their day in Penguin's art department airbrushing cute dreamy covers for a whole range of reprints of everything from Aeschylus to Zola. New books got the same treatment. No matter what the content, every cover somewhere had some butterflies and flowers. Or big smiling suns and fluffy clouds. Or shooting stars. His covers were nothing more than childlike dream worlds created from the nozzle of an airbrush that bore no relation to the book. Alan also created an alphabet of curly serifs that he used on more or less every cover.

This development was noted at the *Eye*. Richard asked me to do a parody of an Aldridge Penguin cover and I chose *Mein Kampf*. I painted Hitler's face as cute and cuddly, like Chaplin's clown. I painted him holding a bunch of flowers and used Aldridge's lettering. It remains one of my favourite parodies.

I met Alan now and again at the Coach and Horses in Greek Street. Alan wasn't a big drinker and was never invited to lunch, but he liked to be seen in fashionable places and at that time the Coach and Horses was fashionable, mainly because Peter Cook could be seen there along with other TV faces. Judi Dench used the Coach when acting in a nearby theatre. So did Peter O'Toole.

Alan and I both found recognition as illustrators around the same time. Alan was picked up by *The Sunday Times* and I got my job on the *Observer* colour magazine. As chance had it, our first commissions appeared on the same Sunday. Our work could not have been more distinctive or different. Alan illustrated a fantasy land, no matter what the subject. I did paintings as I had been taught to at art school. Mainly portraits. Whenever we spoke Alan would tell me about some amazing project he'd cooked up. Once he told me he was in the process of finalising a multi-million-dollar deal with an American sock company. He said he had designed socks for kiddies that had wheels on them and were like little cotton cars. I kept an eye open but nothing like Alan described ever came my way.

Penguin Books were not the only publishers to take drastic steps in an attempt to stave off falling sales. Faber and Faber asked Pete Townshend to take on the job of editing some of their poetry titles. I think they thought that his fans might rush out and buy a slim volume or two of E. E. Cummings. They didn't. They bought 'My Generation'. Penguin Books are now part of Random House. Their books are sold as a commodity alongside coffee mugs, pencil sets, and even deckchairs. But there are no signs of Alan Aldridge's contribution anywhere. What you buy is the design created by the twenty-one-year-old Edward Young in 1935.

Alan died in 2017. He was once asked how he managed to become such a success. I can't help feeling his reply sums up both the man and his contribution to illustration. He said, 'I blag beautifully.'

45

THERE'S A WHOLE SCENE GOING ON

In the early Sixties there were two TV pop music shows. The BBC had *Top of the Pops* and ITV *Ready, Steady, Go!* ITV were leaders by a mile. *RSG!* went out live on Friday, early evening, and opened with the announcement: 'The weekend starts here.' Its success was largely due to the programme's up-to-the-minute style of presentation. The camerawork was sharp. Dancers wore the latest hairstyles and outfits. Brian Eatwell designed the production and commissioned me to design some of the sets. I'd met Brian at Camberwell Art School in 1956. He was fit-looking. Around five foot with straw-coloured curly hair and grey-blue eyes. Nothing escaped his notice. Brian was seldom still, and even when he was, there was always the sense that any second he would be up and on the move again. His nickname was 'The Mighty Atom'. (When Brian moved to Hollywood in the Seventies a mutual friend told me he'd got a Christmas card postmarked Beverly Hills. The message read: 'Love from the Mighty Atom and Raquel.' I used to ask him discreetly about Raquel Welch and he'd give me his bad-boy grin – he had a great bad-boy grin – and let it go at that.) He'd been a member of the National Youth Theatre and had worked with the founder, Michael Croft, learned a lot about acting and designing. Croft's NYT was a major force then and produced a large number of Sixties actors and designers.

For the *RSG!* set I decided to blow up photos of the period and turn them into giant panels that stood freely among the dancers. Leaving aside the audience figures, no matter how hard the BBC tried they never managed to get *TOTP* to look anything other than past it. The gurning, pop-eyed, dyed-blond presence of presenter Jimmy Saville did nothing to help. But the BBC were not to be defeated.

Sometime during 1965, the BBC heads of departments met to discuss the idea of putting out a television magazine show that would act as a genuine rival to *Ready, Steady, Go!* One that would be more than singers miming their latest hit. The BBC's decision was to give the Head of Current Affairs, a man called Paul Fox, the job of sorting out the show, which would go out live after the six o'clock news on Wednesday. It would not have a large budget because the programme would be financed by Current Affairs (meaning not much) rather than light entertainment (meaning millions). The BBC have clear budgetary demarcations. It has a demarcation for everything. Like the army. By placing the new show under the wing of Current Affairs it would mean that the two presenters, one male and one female (to indicate the BBC's sense of gender impartiality), would have to come cheap. No big names with agents demanding fat cheques. The male presenter they got was me. The female they chose was Wendy Varnals. She was a very pretty and mildly ambitious actress who had knocked about with Willie Rushton for a while when they were at Oxford together. The last I heard of Wendy she had run off with Bob Dylan's road manager. Like I say, mildly ambitious.

Paul Fox hired Liz Cowley to produce what was to be called *A Whole Scene Going*, which I think she said was a shortened version of a Bob Dylan line: 'It's a whole scene going on.' Liz was a Canadian journalist with a lot of experience. She put together a pilot which had a Pete Murray lookalike as the presenter. I was invited onto the show to talk about Pop Art.

I was interviewed by Anne Nightingale, who asked me about my work on the set of *Ready, Steady, Go!* I told her I cut up old pop magazines and stuck them to some boards (flats).

A week later I got a call and was asked to present pilot number two with Wendy. Ned Sherrin had seen the pilot and told Paul Fox to dump the bloke with the Brylcremed hair and give the job to Barry, the bloke with long hair and a big nose who looks a bit like Ringo. Ned told Fox: 'Barry is the look of the Sixties.' The BBC took note, and on the first Wednesday in January 1966, *AWSG* went out live to an audience of nine million. By the time it came off air in July, we were watched by over sixteen million.

Liz Cowley was clear from the beginning that she wanted a programme that was different to *RSG!* but that she wanted some of the graphic immediacy of Brian Eatwell's sets. Liz thought, rightly, that the titles would play a big part in telling viewers our show had more to it than a string of pop groups. Liz asked me to do the job and hired film-maker Derek Nice to film the various elements I had in mind that would suggest this was a new kind of pop show. We chose images that would be shown in split-second intervals. These included my collection of toy Japanese robots on the march, my cat looking cute, a rocket being launched, a motorbike being kick-started, all sorts of dolly birds, a bloke pulling a polo neck over his head and a then unknown barefoot Eric Clapton playing a guitar without sound.

Because our budget was so small, getting big names to appear could have proved a problem. But because so many happened to be my mates, I simply asked them, more as a favour than a way of pocketing another couple of grand. Pete, Ray, Manfred Mann . . . they all said yes without thinking.

Twiggy (born Leslie Hornby in Neasden) made her first public appearance on *AWSG* along with her boyfriend and agent, Justin de Villeneuve (born Nigel Davies, not sure where). It was different with American stars as I knew no one from the States, not then anyway. But as the show became more and more popular, big names were less bothered about the fee. They were quite content to be on a show that was big.

Even now I recall Charlton Heston standing modestly in the line of guests waiting to come on. He said it was an honour to be invited when I spoke to him later. His biography, *The Actor's Life*, is well worth a read. He writes honestly about his work and you get a sense of what a dull world the reality of film-making is.

In the first show, I arrived at the studio on a skateboard. No one had even seen a skateboard. Or heard of a skateboard. I looked at the autocue and read out that the skateboard was big on the West Coast and soon you would be able to buy one in the UK for under a pound. I had no idea then, and nor did anyone else, that the skateboard would become as much part of teenage life as rock bands and cheap clothes.

The show ended its run in July and never came back. During the summer break a secret deal had been cooked up between an agent called Bunny Lewis and Paul Fox, who was a silent partner in Lewis's company. Fox fired the entire staff of *AWSG* and got their own people in to run it. They replaced me with Simon Dee and did not find someone to take over from Wendy. Billed as *Dee Time*, the show was stilted and backward-looking, and it transpired that Simon had no gift for interviewing. Christened Cyril Nicholas Henty-Dood, the former public schoolboy had built his reputation as a DJ on the pirate radio ship, *Radio Caroline*. But spinning hits on the high seas is not the same as asking Bill Wyman about his decision to quit the Stones. Or getting Dusty to go further into the reasons for her wild sexually explosive lifestyle. All he did was grin and make silly jokes.

Dee Time was panned by the critics but the BBC carried on regardless. Fox and Lewis did everything they could to make Dee a hit but the public were not having it. After two years of fruitless hype the BBC got rid of him. He took his show to ITV, where it was a giant flop. ITV quickly dropped him and the show. Dee never recovered. He once said, to his credit, 'When the Sixties were over, so was I.'

I often feel the same.

The team at the *Eye* have a private game whereby our death will be reported by the one thing you did that you care nothing about, but for which your name will forever be associated. I am certain that if my death is worth a mention, the headline will read 'SKATEBOARD MAN DEAD'.

46

COSI FANTONI

I got my studio flat at 60 South Side through one of my art teachers. He was called Dick Lee. Dick lived two doors along with his wife Gillian and twin baby daughters. He taught life drawing and composition, and had one of the most kind and generous natures of any men I have ever met. He loved cricket and the sound of jazz. He enjoyed nothing more than asking a few students to his flat, especially during the summer months when we were not at school, to drink bitter bought from the Windmill in large tin jugs and listen to jazz on his old wind-up gramophone. Dick would talk about why Cézanne was the greatest painter of all time because he looked harder than the rest when painting a bowl of apples as well as the chances of England being bowled out before tea.

Dick was born in Rhodesia and served with distinction in the Navy during the war. He was tall with a high forehead and not a lot of hair, and a warm smile was never far away. He drove around in a pre-war Austin Seven that would only go for a mile before something needed to be done to make it go further. Dick never stopped drawing or painting. He would sketch as he talked to you. He drew on anything that came to hand – sketchbooks, the back of an envelope. His flat had white walls that he covered with full-size oil-painted copies of Giotto. He even painted the wooden window shutters and the high walls of the passages. All with images copied from the handful of painters he classed as masters. There was no room for Mondrian or Chagall in Dick Lee's pantheon of painters. Or any others who didn't conform to the principle of remaining absolutely faithful to what you saw. No making it up. Dick Lee's list of greats were Cézanne, Giotto and Rembrandt. It didn't get any longer.

As well as being an extremely kind man, a caring tutor and fine painter, Dick was very funny. More satirical than just jokey. Long before 'found art' became fashionable, Dick would make what he called 'notices' from anything he picked up from dumps or left lying around. Dustbins were his chief supplier. Dick's notices were mostly of people. He did one of me from strands of old wool and string and something long and pointed for my nose. He called it 'Cosi Fantoni'.

A lot of notices were in the form of tongue-in-cheek homages. 'Homage to Picasso' was made from bits of driftwood and old rusty nails and wire just thrown together any old how, yet still it looked like a Picasso. Dick made hundreds during his working life and some still turn up at auctions from time to time. My favourite is 'Homage to Bacon', an assembly which includes an old sardine tin, a dog's rubber bone and the head of a plastic doll. The collection of rubbish is framed by a lavatory seat. I consider Dick Lee's notices as one of the high points in British Art and the forerunners of much of what was to become Sixties Pop Art. And nothing I have seen by the Pop Art generation bettered Dick's notices for wit and originality.

When Dick heard I was looking for a studio he said there was a ground-floor flat at the end of the block, but it had not been lived in for a while and would probably need a lot of work. He gave me the address of the landlord and I went to see him the next day. The address was on Lavender Hill and the landlord looked exactly like Alec Guinness playing Alastair Simm playing the mad Professor Marcus in *The Ladykillers*.

He even wore a long wool scarf and had purple rims round
his eyes. His dingy basement office was lit by gas and filled
with a heavy oak desk littered with piles of receipts and old
rent books. It was right out of Dickens. The rent, he informed
me, was 17/6d (75p) a week. Not much by today's standards,
or Dickens', I suspect. But it was a lot for me. Especially since
I didn't have a regular income. Nevertheless I agreed to take
on the ground-floor flat of 60 South Side. I badly needed a
space to paint and work on my music. I decided that, whatever
the condition, I had enough ingenuity and basic DIY skills to
make the place habitable.

Later in the day I told Sid Steggle, my closest pal at
Camberwell and the drummer in my jazz band, that I had
rented a flat and asked him if he wanted to share with me. He
said that he would be interested and we both went to have a
look.

Dick Lee was right. The place needed a lot of work before
anyone could live there. A lot of the floorboards were missing
and some of the plaster mouldings had come away from the
ceiling. And there was no electricity or gas. Sid and I spent
a month working on the flat and building cupboards from
furniture we picked up from junkshops. We painted the
walls with colours that a company called House & Gardens
produced at the time. We decorated the studio walls white to
help standardise the light, which you need when painting a
picture, and used 'Cantaloupe', 'Thames Green' and 'Blueberry'
for the walls of the second room. These colours became
increasingly fashionable and I have noticed they have been
used again recently, under other names.

Sid's father was a plumber and he sorted out a bath and
two sinks. One wall was in very bad condition so I got some

mail bags (I was working as a temporary postman during the Christmas rush to earn some extra cash) and cut them into sheets. I then glued them to the wall and left them. Their tone was neutral and fitted the look of the place. There was also a problem in that our flat was once part of the basement and the stairs led to it without a door. To have one put in would have been a major job so we talked it over with Eddie, the lady who lived in the basement, to see if we could find a solution. The solution was to do nothing. It didn't bother her and it didn't bother us. And when I got a cat she would make sure Jim got something to eat if I had to spend time away, which I often did.

The funny thing about Jim was that he behaved like a dog. I have even considered that he might have thought of himself as one. When I went into town for the day he would walk from the studio to Clapham Common tube station and wait for me at the top of the stairs. The very first Pop painting I did was of Jim. It was a tribute following his end after a long life. It was part painting and part collage. I took the paper wrapper off a tin of Kitty Cat and stuck it in the corner. I can still remember thinking that this was a big step away from what I had been taught at Camberwell but I had to be led by my instincts. Not my history. I still am.

Not long after we had 60 South Side looking smart, Sid was called up to do National Service. Other art students in Sid's year refused. They became conscientious objectors or worked on farms or in hospitals. Some went to jail. Sid decided it was his duty to serve but deep down I knew he was dreading it. He was a sensitive man. He drew with the insight – and often the sense of humour – that can only come from thinking deeply and feeling deeply. The army changed him as it did millions of others. Sid came home on weekend leave, but not every weekend, and so, in effect, I had the place to myself. As each month passed Sid grew more and more inward-looking. Morose at times. Sometimes he hardly spoke and when I asked him about his life he said blokes would break their legs to get out.

When Sid finally got out of the army he married almost immediately a girl he knew from Camberwell and who he had kept in touch with. The army completely destroyed any ambition Sid had to be an illustrator, and to support his wife and his future large family he took a job as a clerk with Otis elevators, where he worked until he retired. I said at the time that by working for Otis he might go up in the world. Before wasting two years of his life doing National Service, Sid might have laughed.

Had it not been for Dick Lee mentioning that there was an empty flat next to his and Sid Steggle's willingness to share it, one of the few Sixties places for the like-minded to meet would not have existed. And in that case who knows what might *not* have happened?

47

TIME TAKES TIME

Marianne Faithfull was standing alone backstage at the Finsbury Park Empire in North London. I had gone to see Ray and the Kinks. Marianne was booked to close the first half but she had never sung her hit 'As Tears Go By' live. Until then she had only mimed the song when plugging it on the telly. It didn't go well. She forgot the words. Came in too early or too late. Sang in a number of keys – never the key the song was written in. Marianne was in tears. Nerves had got to her. She told everyone within earshot she was not going to do the second show and that she was through with singing live. She'd had enough of showbusiness and that was that.

Clearly it was a crisis. Not to go on again would prove a big disappointment for her thousands of fans. Not to mention her manager and agent and record producer and all the others who had invested a lot of money in making Marianne a star.

I was the nearest to her, so I took the initiative. I told her my name and that what she needed was to sit quietly on her own for a few minutes to settle down. I said I would take her to her dressing room and find her minder, and they could then work out what they would do. She surprised me by saying she had no one with her. Star performers always had someone around to look after them. They got coffee. Made sure the stage dress fitted. Helped with the make-up. I said I would sit with her and she could run through her song with me. Note by note. Word by word. I had no experience of stage fright but I wanted to help. We spent the time together and Marianne went back on and was pretty much perfect.

Following that first encounter we became extremely close. We were never lovers, but in all honesty I can say that I did love her and I think she loved me in her own slightly distant way. We saw each other at least once a week, mainly in her top-floor flat that overlooked Lennox Gardens in Belgravia. She lived with her mother, Eva, who was an Austro-Hungarian baroness. Marianne was in many ways untouched by the wealth her singing had brought her and at that time lived her life outside the excesses and hard drugs of the pop scene. Others were already addicts. But not Marianne. Not yet.

Aged twenty, she loved to entertain socially. Informally. A few close friends. A plain and simple supper party. Her mother would pour chilled white wine and Marianne would knock up a Dover sole with new potatoes. Her close circle of friends included Paul McCartney (a big fan of Dover sole in those days), her record producer Mike Leander, her guitarist Jon Mark and me. Marianne had a charming half-brother called Chris, who was around a lot of the time with a guy called John Dunbar. Chris made movies and John was a bookseller. John was the man Marianne would eventually marry – and then divorce following the birth of their son Nicholas.

Dunbar ran the Indica Gallery with two others: Barry Miles and Peter Asher (Jane's brother). Peter was part of a singing duo called Peter and Gordon who had a hit record called 'A World Without Love'. It was written by Paul McCartney who also had a lot do do with Indica's finances. I think he may have owned it. John met Yoko there at an exhibition of hers in 1966. It was more a place for pop faces to meet than buy anything. But they sold a lot of Hockney etchings. It was another of those Sixties places to be.

During the time we spent together Marianne often spoke about writing her own songs. But she couldn't compose music. I told her that if she gave me a lyric I would write the tune. Or she could ask Paul or her record producer. But she said she would prefer it if I wrote something. I think she felt Paul and Mike might be embarrassed, I don't know. In the event I did the tune. Marianne said there was a poem by Ella Wheeler Wilcox she liked a lot. She took out some lines that would work as a song and handed them over. I then got going on the chords and melody. I set the tempo as a ballad and we called it 'Time Takes Time'. This happened just as Marianne was about to record her second album and she gave the song to Mike Leander. He said he would double the tempo behind her voice to create the sense of time in motion. The album sold millions and for the first time in my life I banked a cheque with three zeros.

We then lost touch until the Eighties. Marianne and Eva had bought Richard Ingrams' small nineteenth-century cottage in Goring-on-Thames (also known locally as Boring-on-Thames, due to the fact that there is nothing there but a pub and a village green) and Richard had moved across the village to a larger version. The green is used for cricket matches and the *Eye* team played there once a year against the local Eleven. I was fielding deep when Marianne suddenly emerged from the tall trees.

'Hello, Barry,' she said. 'I didn't know you played cricket.' I told her that I didn't, that I'd only come to make up the Eleven.

And it was true. Marianne laughed. Her deep open honest laugh. It was a very hot day and she was perspiring heavily and swaying. I thought she was about to faint. It was hard to see the girl I had first met in tears two decades before. She was desperately trying to kick her drug habit and was just about getting there. Her teeth and hair had suffered badly and she was terribly overweight. At first I did not recognise her. But then she smiled and asked how I was. And at once I could see that her warmth and generosity of spirit had not been damaged.

I last saw Marianne a few years back in the garden at the Chelsea Arts Club. She said she was now free of drugs and singing in cabaret, travelling and performing on her own terms. Her home was in Ireland where she had a large house and land.

Marianne is now a strong mature woman. She has experienced tough times yet somehow managed to come through it all. Her voice resonates with a life full of hard knocks and she looks more beautiful than ever. Hard to resist it: time takes time.

48

LIBEL FUNDS AND FLOPPY DISCS

The *Eye* made a lot of money in Sixties. It would have made a lot more had it not been for the libel actions. Richard had a cavalier attitude towards the advice lawyers gave him. Highly qualified men were paid to come into the office on Press Day and read the pages before they were sent off to be printed. Almost every week the lawyers found a story that had the whiff of a libel action. 'If you print this they will sue you,' Richard was warned 'Let them,' was his reply. In some ways I think he almost looked for a case to fight. There was a side to Richard which at that time seemed to relish the drama of a courtroom.

Richard was impressive in the dock. Very much the actor in a leading role. Once, when being cross-examined during the infamous James Goldsmith case, he was asked how he would interpret the Latin phrase *'quid pro quo'*, in relation to an attack the *Eye* had made on Goldsmith following his writ for libel. There was a lengthy dramatic pause before he replied in his clipped patrician accent, 'tit for tat'. (Laughter in court.) When you get under his shield you discover a man who plays Brahms' late works on the piano, has more than a little skill as a painter and has a deep love of the theatre. After reading the Greats at Oxford Richard formed a theatre company named Tomorrow's Audience, which lost money even though the shows were first rate with quality performers. Without a job, so the legend has it, Richard was asked by Rushton and Booker to join them in launching *Private Eye*. This he did, as contributions editor, he became the editor later.

No matter what the outcome, fighting a libel action costs a great deal of money. The *Eye* was always looking for ways to have enough in the bank to fight a case – the libel fund it was called. A sort of war chest. One effective (and amusing) way of bringing in extra revenue was to produce a floppy disc. Floppy discs were very big in the Sixties. They were standard EP/45rpm in format, made from flexible vinyl and not intended to be kept or played for ever. Floppy discs were used mainly by pop groups to plug their latest single with a shelf life of about three weeks. They were stuck to the front covers of pop magazines. At some point, someone at the *Eye* had the idea of recording some *Eye* material onto a floppy disc and sticking it to the cover. A free floppy disc on the cover usually doubled sales since what the reader was getting for free were the talents of Cook, Moore, Humphries, the *Eye* team of Ingrams, John Wells, Willie Rushton, myself and anyone else with a name on the satire scene who was happy to help.

Sometime in 1964 the first floppy was planned and a studio booked. The script was cobbled together from a mixture of recent *Eye* material and Cook improvisations. The immediate problem was that no one had any experience of producing a record, floppy or otherwise. The *Eye*'s first floppy was funny, but the sound was poor and a lot of the jokes got lost under the surface noise and lack of balance. Two floppy discs later, it was clear that a producer was needed.

Because of my work as a jazz musician, I had spent a lot of time in studios and, as more discs were issued, I took control of the production. I found ways of making the music stronger and the voices more distinct. The trick was to provide a more professional recording while preserving something of the *Eye*'s intentionally unprofessional manner. Not slick, in other words. By the mid-Sixties the *Eye* floppy disc had become a regular feature. It would usually be produced to coincide with a major current event, such as joining the Common Market rather than leaving it.

The last floppy disc involved just Peter, John Wells and me. Peter had brought two bottles of Scotch to the session and we drank them both by lunchtime. He then sent someone out for two more. By the end of the recording no one had a clue what we were doing. Me least of all. When I listen to it now I can recognise my alto sax playing 'The Sheik Of Araby' while John does an impersonation of Lord Goodman tap dancing by banging his shoes on the studio's piano lid. The studio was in Soho and at that time there were plenty of prostitutes on the streets. I had a bit of a problem keeping a straight line down Greek Street, and a redhead in a mini skirt said she thought I looked a bit under the weather and would I like to have a lie down. She only lived across the road. She led me up a narrow staircase to her small room. 'Make yourself at home, dear,' she said with a sweet crimson-lipped smile and read out the price list. I said I thought I might just manage the hand job. Alas. Floppy discs. Floppy everything.

When floppy discs were withdrawn, the *Eye* went on to make an LP, *Private Eye's Blue Record*, followed by a single called 'Neasden'. I did the music and Willie wrote every glorious word. 'Neasden' is a tough word to rhyme but it didn't bother Willie. You can hear it in all its discordant splendour on YouTube.

I can't say that libel was an integral part of the Sixties revolution but suing *Private Eye* was. An action against us always made the news. The *Daily Mail* would jump at the chance to inform its readers that snooty irresponsible public schoolboys making fun of the Establishment had been given a slapped wrist. The left-wing *Mirror* usually sided with us. Either way, the publicity attracted readers. People wanted to know what we had said to cause a famous person to sue us.

The most famous case involved Randolph Churchill, who decided to settle out of court after being warned that the publicity would do him no good. Along with paying his costs of £8,000, his legal representative, Peter Carter-Ruck (known to *Eye* readers as Carter-Fuck), forced the *Eye* to offer Churchill an unconditional apology, to be printed on a full page in the *Evening Standard*. It was a bizarre event. The *Eye* reprinted the libel in full and underneath, in very small print, said that we were very sorry. No one on Carter-Fuck's team seemed to notice that we had repeated the libel for the six million *Standard* readers. As a result, our readership more than doubled to 90,000 and Lord Gnome (Ingrams) suggested we might be due a small pay rise.

49

BUSINESS AND PLEASURE

Keith Goodwin was my press agent during the Sixties. His main love was big band jazz and bebop. Not pop. That was his bread and butter. Keith was full of Cockney wit and had the easygoing manner of a radio DJ. The artists he represented were each in their own way a bit quirky, as was Keith himself. Because he liked to talk jazz and knew no one else in the pop world who knew anything about jazz, he suggested that we meet socially. This was unusual because Keith believed adamantly in the old maxim of not mixing business with pleasure. In my case, the rule was easier to break since our backgrounds were similar and I was more a jazz musician than a TV presenter. We had a regular lunch date. Tuesdays at one.

The restaurant where we met was called the London Vega. It was off Leicester Square. When it shut down due to a massive hike in business rates it became an Angus Steakhouse. (Fate: how could you?) The London Vega had genuine Thirties decor – and style. There were tablecloths, silver cutlery and elderly waitresses. One told me George Bernard Shaw was a vegetarian and often dined there when in town for the opening of a new play. His housekeeper listed his dietary requirements in a recipe book which she insisted the restaurant adopt. It was meat and two veg but without the meat. Just cabbage and potatoes. GBS died aged ninety-four when he fell off a ladder while pruning an apple tree. GBS also ate jam sponge and custard, which featured at the top of the dessert menu, followed by Spotted Dick and custard then ice cream (choice of vanilla or strawberry).

I don't think Keith was a vegetarian, but the once fashionable restaurant was rarely full. An overpowering smell of cooked cabbage is not to everyone's taste, so it was easy to find a quiet table where no one would notice a pop personality and his press man. Keith was known to be secretive in his dealings but he was always open with me. During those lunches I learned a lot about him, the people he represented and the way he ran his business.

Dusty Springfield was his most famous client. The first time Keith and I lunched together he said, 'My job will be getting your name into the newspapers. Same as it is to keep Dusty's out.' It was not generally known then that Dusty was gay, and any mention of it was likely to seriously damage her reputation. Keith had his hands full as Dusty was a serious drug user and had a string of casual affairs. This is common knowledge now but at the time Keith made sure that Dusty was presented to the public as straight. Short skirts. Big kohl-rimmed eyes. Blonde hair. The works. Her audience was eighty per cent male, and Keith wanted to keep it that way.

Keith had a routine for getting the material he used to promote his less troublesome clients. He would phone up and ask for news. Anything. Whatever you told him, no matter how trivial, Keith would always find an angle to turn it into a news story. One morning he called and I told him I had a terrible sore throat. The midday edition of the *Evening Standard* ran a story plus pic with the heading, 'TV's Barry in Throat Cancer Scare'. The report told how I had been kept in a private hospital overnight following the discovery of a suspicious lump in my throat. It went on to say that tests had found nothing more serious than a viral infection and I had been discharged with a clean bill of health. (The name of the hospital was not mentioned.)

Keith's office was in Manette Street, just round the corner from the *Eye*. Keith looked after the press interests of Donovan, Cat Stevens, The Temperance Seven, Johnny Kidd, P. J. Proby, top motorcyclist Barry Sheene, the Ryan Twins and Dusty. Apart from Barry Sheene, I knew all Keith's other clients.

The Ryan Twins were the sons of the singer Marian Ryan. Marian starred in a telly show called *Spot the Tune* which ran from 1956 to 1962. It was worth watching for her alone. She was a vivacious woman who wore expensive clothes and expensive perfumes, and the press dubbed her something like 'The British Marilyn Monroe of Song'. And, as they also said, 'she oozed sex'. When her twins became hit makers she went everywhere with them. When they were on *AWSG* Mum sat proudly watching from the front row – the show was transmitted live in front of an audience. One of the Ryans wrote a hit for Frank Sinatra and one died from cancer while in his forties. When Marian's telly show finally folded, and having divorced the twins' father in the meantime, the Marilyn Monroe from Middlesborough married a multi-millionaire and went to live happily ever after in Miami.

Cat Stevens was born into a Greek family. He was christened Steven Demetre Georgiou but changed his name as he though 'Cat' sounded catchy. More like a pop singer's name than Steven. When Cat decided Islam suited him better than Greek Orthodoxy he ditched Cat and became Yusuf. His big hit was 'Matthew And Son' – possibly the only one of his hits anyone can remember. He has Keith to thank for the title.

Keith's office overlooked a hardware store called Matthew & Son. One day they were wracking their brains for an offbeat song title that would catch the public's imagination, in the way 'Waterloo Sunset' and 'Winchester Cathedral' had done. The song itself is little more than the title repeated over and over. Keith got up from his desk and looked out the window. Suddenly he noticed the name of the hardware store across the street. Matthew & Son. Bingo! The story sounds like an urban myth but not so. Keith told me himself over a tepid sponge pudding and vegan ice cream at one of our lunches.

I never knew Johnny Kidd but I got on really well with his drummer, Clem Cattini. He was Anglo-Italian like me and his family ran restaurants, as did mine. When Johnny Kidd (born Freddy Albert Heath) died in a car crash, Clem went solo and became a top session drummer. He was first choice for everyone from Tom Jones to the Walker Brothers. I was fortunate to have Clem drumming on all the solo records I made at that time.

Keith presented Donovan as Britain's answer to Bob Dylan. A loner. A young Rabbie Burns wrapped up in his own spiritual world. A seeker of truth, freedom and beauty through the simple things of life. But apart from a handful of hits, Don didn't go as far as everyone thought he would. There was never going to be another Dylan. Don is still around. Still trying to catch the wind.

I tried to like Dusty. But I couldn't. And she didn't care. She found men hard going, especially men who fancied her. And a lot did. But you needed to know Dusty off stage to get the real picture. To see the face beneath the heavy make-up, back-combed hair and black eyeliner. What I saw was a rather frightened and plain-looking girl from the London suburbs with a bad temper and a desperate need to be loved.

After a while, Keith gave up being a press agent and became a manager. He moved to Malta where he wrote books on jazz and pop and anything else that took his fancy. He died in 2004, five years after Dusty.

50

FANTONI FANS

AWSG had been running about three months and the BBC were getting a lot of fan mail which they sent on to the office. Sacks full. It was unexpected and it needed a decision: what to do with it? The answer was simple. The time had come, so my managers Geoff and Pete told me, to start a fan club. A fan club? Were they serious? They were. Everyone on telly who had anything to do with the Swinging Sixties had a fan club. Big names hired staff to run them. They were paid to fake the Big Star's signature on photos and send printed letters with the same answer to whatever question was sent. Some fan clubs were official, based in big offices. Others were run by small groups of fans from kitchen tables.

Geoff and Pete had no resources to hire staff to deal with my mail and they had no experience of fan clubs either. But their instinct was right. As daft as it sounded, I needed a fan club. The piles of letters would have to be answered. If anyone had taken the trouble to write to me, no matter who and no matter the subject, the least I could do was find the time to reply. Someone would have to run the Barry Fantoni Fan Club. But who? Geoff asked his wife but she couldn't type. Peter would have asked his wife but he didn't have one at the time. I asked a few of my girlfriends but none of them were interested in what Annie from Aberdeen thought about my smile. Finally a solution was found, and from an unexpected source.

On Sundays when I was free I always tried to have lunch with my mum and dad. It was a way to catch up. During the telly years my mum would often give lunch to some of my pop mates who were from the same background and aware of the importance of family ties, obligations and rituals. She got to know and like quite a few of them, especially Ray Davies, and saw them as her own friends as much as mine. She also liked all my *Eye* mates, in particular Christopher Booker, who often joined us for Sunday lunch. In return, we would spend New Year with Christopher and his family in the West Country, where his parents ran a private school for girls.

My parents' flat was on the top floor of Dumbarton Court, a fine example of mid-Thirties architecture that overlooked London from the brow of Brixton Hill. On a clear day you could see across the valley to Primrose Hill. It was a magnificent view and I painted it frequently when I lived there. I liked painting it best at night, from the balcony. You could see where the Thames cut the capital in half by the line of illuminated buildings. The OXO Tower. The Shell Building. St Paul's, which had just been floodlit for the first time. Dumbarton Court was sold to Lambeth Council in the Eighties and allowed to rot under the political criminals who were in charge.

When I told my mum about the fan club and the need of a club secretary she said she would like to give it a go. My mum, who everyone called Max, was fifty-seven at the time and had a full-time job managing her brother George Dee's betting shop in Brixton. Max had learned to touch type before she was married and had done a lot of secretarial work over the years. She even had a small portable typewriter and a space to store the things we would need. I wasn't sure. It was a lot of work, but Max would not take no for an answer.

I was secretly delighted as I knew she would do a professional job. Geoff and Pete were equally delighted. A plan was drawn up. We decided to charge fifteen shillings a year. For that a member got the following: one red-and-white lapel badge, a personally signed photo and and a monthly newsletter with dates of my appearances at supermarket openings and concerts and anything else that seemed newsworthy. The first newsletter highlighted my debut tour as a solo singer, scheduled to coincide with the release of my first single, 'Little Man In A Little Box' – the song Ray had written for me. I went on tour with the Spencer Davis Group and my band closed the first half.

Max enjoyed corresponding with fans and spent a lot of time with those who she thought had more to say than just a few words of praise. She always signed off the letters 'Max, Club Secretary'. As a result, there was to be an unexpected turn of events. One young girl seemed to be in a lot of difficulty. Janet wrote weekly about her unhappy home life. Her mother had recently died and her father was seldom home. She had two younger brothers, and all three spent a lot of time living in her aunt's house. Max became a surrogate mother to this teenager. As time passed they became pen friends. The girl eventually married and had children.

Going through Max's things after she died, I found a card-board box with 'FAN CLUB' written on the side. Max had kept all the personal letters fans had sent to her. Many hundreds. I found Janet's letters. They were full of thanks and appreciation for all Max's help. And there were photos of her and her husband. The baby. Janet at school. Janet outside a church.

Being on the telly helped me in many ways but it also did a lot of damage. It gave me a false impression of myself. It does to most people who go on the box. But it was a big help to Janet. She said as much in every fan letter. I looked at the pictures and read Janet's letters, thinking that the whole telly thing was probably worth it for that single pen-friendship alone. And writing this now, I see no reason to change that view.

51

CLICK, CLICK, EVERY TRIP

Until the early Sixties the only photographers who got serious press attention were those who took pictures of the rich and famous. Cecil Beaton was a good example. He photographed debutantes in country mansions wearing expensive hats made by his colourful pals in Mayfair. The son of a wealthy timber merchant, Cecil took hundreds of photos of Her Majesty the Queen and her family and quite a few are actually in focus. Karsh of Ottawa was another name the public knew. He rose to fame by taking snaps of Hemingway, JFK, Churchill and the young Queen Elizabeth. The old school used cameras with plates. The new school were happy with an Olympus Trip. The camera of the Sixties. The one used by David Hemmings in Antonioni's baffling film *Blow-Up*, which had a photographer as the focus, so to speak.

Through my work as an illustrator and being part of the social scene I got to know most of them. Terry Donovan best. Terry was a good pal and a great photographer. His work was sharp and immediate. His portraits are full of wit. I asked him to be a guest on *AWSG*, along with Twiggy and her agent Justin de Villeneuve. Terry was Twiggy's principal photographer and entirely responsible for establishing her look.

Until Twiggy arrived on the fashion scene Jean Shrimpton was considered to be the Face of the Sixties. The Sixties fashion world insisted on having 'a face' and by 1966 it had grown just a little weary of the Shrimp. A new face was wanted and the face they got was Twiggy's. Terry added emphasis to her big wide eyes and built her look around them. He made the most of her slender neck, freckles, Sassoon crop and her fresh, at times boyish beauty. On full-length shots Terry didn't hide Twiggy's twiggy legs. He made a feature of them. You have only to see photos of Lesley Hornby before she became Twiggy to see the dramatic changes Terry made to her look.

Terry was a lot of fun. He was a big man. Stout and never without a smile or witty remark, he was a master of patter. He spent his evenings eating in expensive restaurants and drinking fine wines. Apart from pop stars, I knew few people who earned more for a day's work. But I knew few who spent what they earned so freely. And enjoyed spending it so much. Like a lot of my mates from that time, Terry had also been born in Stepney, and this did a lot to seal our friendship. Terry talked a lot about where he had been born – the places he remembered with affection. Holding a glass of claret, eyes glazed over, he'd rattle them off like a Cockney litany.

'St Dunstan's. A thousand years old. The Church of the High Seas it's called because of the shipbuilders who lived around there. The Whitechapel Bell Foundry. Old as the hills. Best bells in the world. They put the bells into St Dunstan's. You sing them in "Oranges And Lemons". The bells of Stepney. We all got taught that when we were kids. Blooms. Just across the road from the foundry. Open all hours. Chicken soup and salt beef. The Yiddish Theatre. Brick Lane and a stool for everything. Better than Harrods and cheaper by half. The pet market one street along from Brick Lane. Only open Sunday mornings. Leman Street and the shop that never closed. Never. Run by a Pakistani and his son. Sidney Street. Where they had the siege. Where Sid Smollett had a workshop that made high-class ladies' underwear.'

A year after Terry appeared on *AWSG* with Twiggy and Justin, he opened his own restaurant on the Fulham Road. Terry called it Trenchermen's – meaning a hearty eater. After a glitzy first night, when the place was packed with Sixties celebrities, business quickly dropped off. The problem was typical of the time. Once someone had established themselves in one field, they thought they could do the same in another. And some did. Some of the most influential figures of the Sixties were well known for their skills across the board. Bowie was a more than credible actor. Dudley acted, sang and played the piano. But Terry was a photographer and not even a tenth-rate restaurateur. In less than a year Trenchermen's closed and it hurt Terry more than he admitted. Gradually the façade of the tubby genial Terry began to crumble and he became a very different man to the one I had first met when he came on *AWSG*. He killed himself in 1996. The coroner put Terry's suicide down to depression.

Brian Duffy is also dead. We met when he was taking pictures for the prestigious Pirelli calendar. I knew the art director who commissioned me to write copy for the calendar. If pushed, I would say that Duffy's photos are the most enduring. I know that a fashion picture is not intended to be much more than an ephemeral image of an ephemeral subject and that its success is in presenting a sense of immediacy and, to some degree, excitement, but Duffy had an edge. His images were less about surface. More about what lay beneath. His picture of John Lennon is all about Lennon. Not what John thought about himself or what Duffy was trying to add on. I consider David Bailey to be the better fashion photographer and Terry more offbeat. But Duffy's pictures were the deepest.

Bailey is the name most people think of when it comes to Sixties photography. And not only for his pictures. His affairs were never a secret. I never came across Bailey socially or professionally as I was not a female fashion model, and he spent most of his time, day and night, with female fashion models. I was told by someone who knows him that he was prone to remark, 'Fifty years ago I'd drive across London for a shag. Now I send my assistant.' He was paid to promote the Olympus Trip camera, which he used to great effect on the likes of the Shrimp.

There were other Sixties photographers whose work I'd rank with the very best. I would include Jane Bown's intimate portraits and Harri Peccinotti's erotic close-ups of glossy lipsticked mouths at the very top. Neil Libbert's pictures taken at theatrical performances set a new standard. Terry O'Neill married Faye Dunaway and still had time to take photos of pop stars. His early picture of Mick Jagger having his hair combed in a TV make-up room is one of my favourite images of the Stones frontman. Terry is a member of the Chelsea Arts Club and we meet there from time to time and discuss what it was like to walk down the King's Road when it had proper pubs and no tourists.

Don McCullin is without question one of the greatest war photographers of all time. We would sometimes eat lunch together in a narrow snack bar run by Israelis off the Charing Cross Road. He had seen some of the most terrible things that human beings can do to each other and sometimes his face would show it. But most of the time he had plenty of good tales to counteract the bad ones. His modesty was only matched by his genius.

Lewis Morley did a lot more than take a picture of Christine Keeler sitting naked astride a chair. His pictures of emerging

Sixties stars such as Michael Caine, Donovan and the *Beyond the Fringe* foursome of Cook, Moore, Miller and Bennett are masterpieces of portrait photography. Lewis was a very close friend, even though he went to live in Australia. He was eighty-eight when he died in 2013, largely due to a broken heart following the death of his wife three years earlier. This paragraph from the *Guardian*'s obituary says much.

> Morley's friendship with Cook made him a regular photographic contributor to *Private Eye* in its early days. He produced spoof portraits ('Spotty Muldoon' wearing a brown paper bag over his head) and fashion photographs such as *The Loony Look* (1967), featuring Willie Rushton, Barry Fantoni and Diana Clarke satirising fashions of the day by posing in army surplus clothes.

Morley also worked on genuine fashion shoots for magazines such as *She* and *Harper's Bazaar*. Notably, Lewis took the first published photographs of Jean Shrimpton for *Go!* magazine in 1961. Another first were his photographs of Twiggy in an old fur coat, published in *London Life* magazine in 1965, well before Terry became her main photographer.

For a long time I thought that the Sixties revolution more or less happened at once. That the Beatles, Pop Art and the pictures Bailey took of Shrimpton in New York for *Vogue* all began at the same time. But this was not the case. The David Bailey/*Vogue* session was in 1960. Pop Art was next to grab the young public's imagination along with *Private Eye* in 1961. Pop Art's big breakthrough was the result of an exhibition put on by 'The Young Contemporaries' at the RBA gallery in 1962. This was mainly a closed-shop show of work by Royal College students including Hockney, Blake and so on. It wasn't until late 1962, six months after the Pop Art show, that the Beatles' 'Love Me Do' made the Top Ten, followed by 'Please, Please me' in March 1963 and then 'She Loves You' in August.

At this point the Sixties officially arrived.

52

WILLIE RUSHTON'S GRANNY'S KITCHEN

The *Private Eye* office was often quite empty in the early days, especially during the week following Press Day (the *Eye* being a fortnightly lampoon.) There were just the girls and two chaps sorting out the admin. Now and then Dr Jonathan Miller would drop in. He had no reason to call apart from to sit in the middle of the office and talk non-stop while waving his arms about. He considered himself an entertaining and perceptive wit. A man of culture who had read widely and was capable of great things. We were always pleased to see him head for the door. In later years Dr Miller became Dr Johnson in one of the funniest parodies the *Eye* ever produced. Written in the style of Samuel Johnson, Miller's antics as a director of operas and the like were chronicled by John Boswells – an in-house attack on contributor John Wells. The *Eye* always makes fun of its own. A class thing. Upper and lower. We all got it in the neck at one time or another from one of our chums.

As the Sixties moved on, the *Eye* slowly regained a lot of the readers it had lost as a result of satire hitting a dip. At one point we were selling less than 15,000 copies an issue. Cook was at the heart of the satire revival as he had been in its conception, and his appearances with Dud on the telly in *Not Only . . . But Also* gave the *Eye* a new and younger audience. Ian's razor-sharp contributions to *Have I Got News for You* have much the same effect on the *Eye*'s readership figures today. We added more pages (from eight to twenty-four) and Richard hired a handful of new contributors. Bernard Levin had a bash. Bernard was a theatre critic and had a spot on

TW3 doing in-depth interviews with people suspected of dodgy dealings. He became famous overnight for enraging an actor called Desmond Leslie, who thumped Bernard on the nose for giving his actress wife a damning review.

Bernard's stint on the *Eye* did not last more than a few issues. His style was just a little pompous, like the man himself. You can never be really funny if you take yourself too seriously. He later opened London's first cartoon gallery on Gloucester Road with the actor and TV music pundit Robin Ray. I showed there. All the *Eye*'s cartoonists did until the gallery closed due to poor sales. No one will pay much for a cartoon drawing, no matter how brilliant, but they'll spend a small fortune on a Hockney etching, no matter how poor.

Robin was a very nice man who lived with his lovely wife, Susan, a TV presenter, in Brighton. Bernard was always a good host at private views. His pompous pose gave way to a warm and social soul who could be very funny when he wanted. At the age of forty-one, Bernard fell in love with a young Greek lady called Arianna Stassinopoulos (now Huffington). She wanted very much to help Bernard find a religion that satisfied him as much as listening to and writing about Wagner. She did not succeed and Bernard died in 2004 without embracing any recognised faith. At his memorial service, Sir David Frost announced that 'Bernard was a great crusader. Remember always that the pen is mightier than the sword – and easier to write with.' The groans were audible.

Thirties communist author and journalist Claud Cockburn was given a full page to fill every week. He was nearing sixty when he began to contribute to the *Eye*. He had been a soldier in the Spanish Civil War and lived in Ireland. Claud was an eccentric as well as a fine writer, and he drank a fair bit when the mood took him. Which was most of the time. This hindered his sense of timing. His copy never arrived when it was expected and very often he would end up reading it down the line. This took hours because Claud's speech was garbled, even when sober. When asked why his copy had not arrived, Claud's answers were unforgettable. Dreamlike at times. My favourite was that he had left the finished copy on his desk, which was in front of an open window. He had gone to put the kettle on to make a cup of tea before nipping down to the village post office to buy a stamp but when he came back into the room a chicken suddenly jumped in the window, picked up the sheets of paper in its beak and took off down the garden where it vanished into a hedge. Along with his copy.

When Claud wrote his memoir, he asked me to do the cover. The title was *Through a Broken Window*. The cover I designed was made from a full-size window which had a broken pane of glass at the bottom. A photo of Claud stuck behind it stopped the elements getting in. His publisher Penguin used the photo but nothing else and called the book *I, Claud*. We both hated the cover.

John Wells then joined the team. John had been teaching in public schools after leaving Oxford and hadn't been enjoying it. John was fond of nights out with pretty girls and lots to eat and drink. There was a distinct lack of all three at Rugby. His contributions were to be of major importance, co-writing with Richard on 'Mrs Wilson's Dairy' and later 'Dear Bill'. John died from a brain tumour in 1998. It should never have happened. The tumour was missed following a scan twelve years previously. Had it been detected, the tumour could have been removed and John would still be alive. A man from the *Daily Mail* phoned to tell me that John had died. It was a

Sunday morning and he asked me for a quote. I said that I had spoken to John a week ago and we had talked about the work we had done together and how our friendship had deepened over the years. Something like that. Shock reduces most of us to talking on autopilot.

Had I been given more time I might have mentioned that John had a very interesting philosophy when it came to travel. When he travelled alone, he would always stay at the cheapest hotel available. If he had a lady with him, he would stay at the best. When we worked together for a month in Spain on a screenplay David Niven had commissioned, John rented a single room in a tiny hotel built on the end of a marina. It had a bed. A chair. A washbasin. A window. He drank beer and ate sardines from a tin. When his girlfriend joined us for a week, he moved to the only five-star hotel in town and ordered lobster and champagne. I learned a lot from John.

It was also about this time that the Labour MP for Barking Tom Driberg began doing the *Eye* crossword. Driberg was a notorious homosexual and close friend of the criminals Ronnie and Reggie Kray. He was an amusing man for all his odious dealings with young boys and guardsmen in the bushes of St James's Park. Although Tom knew all about the cover-ups and scandals in high places – how both the Tories and Harold Wilson kept quiet about the vile Lord Boothby's association with the Krays and rent boys – he failed to tell the *Eye*. A sign, I consider now, to be of one of his many failings. In time Tom became more than a crossword compiler and I found myself working with him on a strip that ran for many years called 'Focus on Fact'. Tom had plenty of facts about everyone. Only he was careful about which ones he let slip.

A man called Tariq Ali once told me he was a contributor. He was always hanging around the office, but as far as I could see he contributed nothing and I never quite understood how he got in. I think he said he was a member of the Socialist Workers Revolution Party, which was Paul Foot's bag. Tariq, I was to discover, came from a wealthy Pakistani family with a long history of preaching left-wing politics and revolutionary ideals. Tariq would turn up early and seldom leave until everyone went home. He just sat around all day, laughing loudly at Ingo's jokes and getting in the way. A whole bunch of time wasters made themselves at home at that time. Gossipmongers, mainly. Slicker, a man who drove a yellow sports car, was one. Fleet Street hacks who played up to Richard's weakness for a tawdry tale. I remember doing a poster of Tariq for the *Eye* when it parodied some demo or other. The brief was to make him look like Lenin.

Christopher Booker was the last of the original joke team to go into the office to write as part of the team. He did so with Ian, forming a unique collaboration of the first editor and the current editor. In 2018 Christopher was diagnosed with pancreatic cancer. The last time we met, just after New Year, it was clear that the fighting spirit he used to edit the first ever copy of *Private Eye* in 1961 had not diminished. Ian and I went together. The day was perfect. A clear blue sky and the hilly landscape filled with stone buildings and farm animals grazing was lit by an ethereal golden light. Christopher's home was the rectory, next door to the church. An orchard behind a crumbling brick wall at the end of the long garden. We lunched in the old pub.

Christopher died peacefully at his home in Litton, on 3 July 2019, having given a short speech about the everlasting nature of love, surrounded by his loving family.

He was a rare man. Honest and noble. A campaigner at heart, with just a touch of the Victorian Christianity that had led many of his uncles to become bishops and archbishops. One of them gave up his flock for the job of Governor of the Bank of England and picked up £80,000 a year. Eight million today. There is a picture of him hanging on the staircase wall. Christopher would shake his head in dismay when telling the story. But smile openly when telling how another uncle had scored a goal for Oxford in the 1874 Cup Final. Oxford 2 Royal Engineers 0.

Sitting discussing the hymns he wanted for his funeral service was a long way from the heady atmosphere of the Sixties Revolution. The early years when we both worked together three days a fortnight and attacked the Establishment, and in the case of exposing the Profumo affair, managing to bring down a government. But as he repeated his much-told story about sticking the pages of the very first copy of *Private Eye* together on the floor of Willie Rushton's granny's kitchen it was obvious that that moment in history remained deeply important to him. And so it should. Without Christopher's energy, grasp of dates and facts, not to mention his very unusual sense of humour, the *Eye* would not have existed. I believe that without *Private Eye*, the spirit of the Great Cultural Revolution would have been very lop-sided. A humourless business made up of no more than pop songs, paintings of Elvis and dolly birds in mini skirts.

53

POP!

In 1963 images of the Beatles were everywhere. Like their music, inescapable. Look in any shop window – and not just the record shop on the high street (when high streets had record shops) – and the Fab Four would be there, smiling back at you. It didn't matter which window: Woolworths, the Co-op, Boots, Dolcis, the Westminster Bank, Timothy White. There they were. John, Paul, George and Ringo. With their Beatle fringes and silver crew-neck suits. Yet oddly, only two official publicity shots were available in 1963. One was a black-and-white full-length group shot and the other was a colour image.

The colour image was printed on handbills as well as on cardboard for window displays. It showed only the heads and was so badly cropped that Ringo only just made it into the right-hand side. The picture was printed on cheap paper at speed, which caused the colour separations to print slightly off-register. This produced a thin red line around the heads, as if a toddler had used a pencil to drawn an outline. This appealed to me. The poor print quality shifted the image from being just another publicity shot. It was already something of an artwork. When I painted a picture of the Beatles from the handbill in oil on canvas, a little larger than life-size, I decided to retain the off-register red line around their heads. It stopped it from being just another homage.

Since the Beatles were a performing band I chose to paint the picture as a performance. The AIA Gallery (now defunct) in Lisle Street gave me the ground-floor gallery. I set up my easel and put a portable hi-fi on the floor next to my paints. While playing Beatles records I painted the picture in public, as if it were a live performance. I gave out the times when I would be working and people came to watch. The canvas took a week to complete and I have been told by many that it was the very first painting of the Beatles. But I am not sure. I think Peter Blake might have beaten me to it by a month. No matter.

Both pictures broke new ground. No one had seriously painted a pop group before then. Not even Elvis. Andy Warhol's *Elvis* came later. Once I had finished and the paint was dry, I hired a van and sent it to a number of public and private galleries throughout Britain. The painting was on tour for a year and opened in a gallery in Liverpool, one as near to the old Cavern Club as possible. Not long after the painting went on tour, I met Paul for the first time. Without red lines round his face. It was 1964, at the New Cavendish Gallery (now also defunct).

The show was a mix of Pop Art and less trendy pieces. All nicely painted. Landscapes and seascapes. I had put in a few pieces that I hadn't included in my Woodstock show. Paul knew of the painting I had done of the Beatles, and about it going on tour, but didn't buy this picture until much later in our friendship. The work he took home from the New Cavendish was called *Ducks in Flight*. It was a recreation of a Fifties suburban living-room wall covered in tasteless wallpaper and three plaster ducks hanging one under the other. The classic hanging position for ducks in flight is to have the top duck a little ahead of the second duck and the second duck a little ahead of the third duck, which is how I hung them.

I saw more of Paul when he bought his house at the back of Lord's cricket ground. We had a routine. I would drive to St John's Wood and then we would either spend time at his home talking about painting or the latest trends in songwriting. Or he'd come to Clapham and check out what I was doing. On the way we might drop in to see Marianne Faithfull in her flat in Lennox Gardens.

One July evening at Marianne's place, Paul was sitting on the sofa trying to tune her very old and unloved guitar while she was in the kitchen cooking him a sole with lemon sauce. Her future husband John Dunbar was pouring out wine and I think Jon Mark was there. A fine guitarist, laid-back, he arranged a lot of Marianne's material. And her mother. She was always there. Marianne didn't go in for hi-fi. She listened to records on a small cheap portable record player she'd got from Woolworths. There were piles of records scattered all over the flat. She had a copy of the Kinks' 'See My Friends' which had just been released. Ray had written it years before while on a trip to India. Paul was listening very carefully. He kept playing it and I could tell he was making mental notes.

The words are quite abstract, and over the years have been the subject of much analysis. Are these friends gay? What kind of friends, if not? Paul was not interested in the words. What he latched on to was the sitar sound of Dave's guitar in the background. I sensed he could hear something in it he had not heard before. The next time the Beatles had a date at Abbey Road (December of the same year, 1965), they recorded 'Norwegian Wood', complete with a sitar that sounds remarkably like Dave's guitar on 'See My Friends'.

It is well known that Paul and John only collaborated during the early years. Paul's songs were pretty. John wrote as a poet.

His songs have more than one dimension. 'Strawberry Fields' is a good early example. By contrast, the Kinks' songs come only from Ray's inner world. His poetical vision is unique to his personal history. Authentic. 'See my friends, playin' across the river . . .' These are words that open the imagination. That suggest images. Don't explain them.

In the middle of the Sixties, David Hockney started making etchings and got a studio to print limited editions. His adoring public gobbled them up. Suddenly print dealers, who had experienced some lean times since the print heyday of the Thirties, were back in business. They sold signed Hockney etchings for the price of a new washing machine and no Swinging Londoner's home was complete without both. Hockney's prints were pretty to look at. Easy on the eye. Bland, perhaps. But not all. One image was of David sitting naked, facing Picasso. David said it was an homage to Picasso, who was a great printmaker (and who didn't print his own plates either). Rembrandt and Goya were also both master etchers. I could name a hundred more. But Pablo had them all beat. His breadth of vision and invention of a new visual language is the reason. Just to think of it. A new visual language. It is akin to building a Mac from an abacus single-handed.

No one at the *Eye* could take Hockney's work seriously, apart from layout man Tony Rushton. He bought one of the prints very early on and didn't pay all that much. A hundred maybe. When he sold it twenty years later he bought a vast Victorian house in South London with the profit. Ingrams renamed Hockney 'Cockeye'. It was about then that the *Eye* ran a strip about bachelors called 'The Gays' in which everyone was terribly sad. It was the first strip Hislop dropped when he became editor.

In the wake of Hockney making a killing with cross-hatching and 'cool' fashionable images, a whole bunch of new printmakers sprang up. Artists who decided to ditch their brushes and canvas for the etching needle and a copper plate. The shop where they got their materials was called T.N. Lawrence & Son. It was in a backwater of Clerkenwell called Bleeding Heart Lane. Stanley Lawrence was in his nineties when the etching boom hit the art world. He was never easy to get on with. His manner was terse, and as he aged he lost his hearing and much of his sight. But old Stan Lawrence knew the etching game inside out. He stocked everything a printmaker would ever need. A roll of blanket for the press. Acids of all sorts. Beeswax to burn over the copper. Ask Stan for a specific mezzotint rocker and he'd potter off in his brown warehouse coat to the storeroom and come back with a box full. Each of them different.

I had known him from my days studying printmaking at Camberwell and he once told me that before a Hockney print mounted in a slender aluminium frame became a Sixties craze he had been about to shut down. But thanks to Hockney and his etchings, T.N. Lawrence & Son kept their doors open. They now have branches the world over.

Screenprinting had also become popular. But the images had a flat look, which was fine if you were using a screen to print a supermarket price ticket or a sign for new potatoes, but if you wanted a top quality print that wasn't an etching you used lithography. An image printed from a stone. Greek. *Litho* – stone. *Graph* – image. Toulouse-Lautrec's famous posters of the Moulin Rouge were printed on litho presses.

If you wanted a quality lithograph printed in the Sixties you went to the Curwen Press. The man who ran it was called Andrew Purchase. He lived with his wife and young baby in a perfectly maintained early Victorian house in the middle of Stockwell Green. Because Andrew lived two stops away on the Northern Line we saw a lot of each other and he would often come to 60 South Side for a chat and to see what I was up to.

One morning in the summer of 1966 he dropped by as I was finishing an illustration for the *Melody Maker*'s spin-off monthly called *Music Maker*. It was a head and shoulders of Bob Dylan wearing shades with stars in the lenses. I had Bob smoking a joint and filled the space around him with planets like you see in images of a galaxy. Andrew liked it a lot. He said that as long as I had the publication rights (which I always insisted on) he would print it as a three-colour lithographic poster. All I needed to do was to make the colour separations and choose the colours. I chose red and yellow and the image of Bob was in black and white. We printed a couple of hundred and within weeks a couple of hundred more. It was like having a hit record. It was not long before we were selling thousands.

With Bob Dylan making the charts on paper as well as vinyl we decided to do a follow-up poster. I painted Al Capone. For the background I used a photo of a gangster's moll. A blonde. I placed twenty-four small identical pictures side by side, which created a decorative pattern, a bit like wallpaper. The blonde in the photo had a Twenties-period face complete with cute bow lips and big eyes. Jenny was the girlfriend of drummer Aynsley Dunbar. He was yet to make a name for himself and spent most of his time stoned. Drums didn't feature a lot in

Aynsley's life and I am astonished that he did so well given his earlier lack of enthusiasm for practising the traps.

Al Capone was also a hit but Bob in his shades smoking pot was the poster everyone wanted. It had been on sale for six months and selling fast when I got a call from a pop group manager (the name has gone) who said he had signed the singer Linda Lewis. She was seventeen. He asked me to make a dress out of the Dylan poster for Linda to wear in publicity shots. It was a first. I had helped to make suits out of worsted, serge, tweed, wool and linen. But never a dress out of a poster. I fancied the challenge so I agreed and made the dress by wrapping a couple of posters around Linda in her undies and 'stitching' them with pins and Sellotape.

Linda Lewis was very bright and knew a lot about music at all levels. To thank me she gave me a book about Beethoven. It was inspirational. Until then I had known nothing about the man, but reading about his deafness, depression and musical vision, I was overwhelmed by his tenacity and genius. I spent the next five years on a life-size portrait of Beethoven standing on Clapham Common. I used the common because it was outside my window and I had never been to Vienna.

Beethoven played a very big part in my life. After I completed the picture in 1970 it was displayed in the foyer of the Royal Festival Hall during the festival celebrating the two-hundredth anniversary of his birth. The *Observer* colour magazine used the head on the cover in their tribute to Beethoven the same year. It was then featured in *Graphis*, a German monthly devoted to illustration.

In time poster art outgrew its Sixties Pop Art origins and became a vehicle for expressing a wide variety of images, not all of them pandering to fashion. The poet Christopher

Logue, who invented the 'True Stories' feature in the *Eye* invented the poster poem. His posters sold in thousands. The poster that sold the most was titled 'I Shall Vote Labour'. I have a copy on my wall. You can see Christopher reading it on YouTube.

54

PENNY AND CHRISTINE

There were a lot of new magazines in the wake of the Beatles selling eighty million records a year. Other bands like the Stones, the Searchers, Billy J. Kramer and Gerry and the Pacemakers added on another hundred million single sales. These new magazines were aimed squarely at teenage girls and they bred a whole new generation of young female writers to fill the pages of *Jackie, Pop, Fabulous, Oh Boy, Seventeen* and all the rest. If you got a job working on a girls' teenage weekly you mainly rewrote press releases and storylines for cartoon strips that told the reader how Manfred Mann tore his hair out when Paul Jones went solo and how he got over it when he discovered Mike d'Abo. And you would have to do a lot of interviews. These mags carried a lot of what-I-had-for-breakfast interviews. One day you would be talking to Kenny 'Up On The Roof' Lynch, who might not have a lot to say about his breakfast. The next, Keith Moon who would be too out of it to say anything, least of all how he liked his boiled eggs.

Penny Valentine worked at *Disc*. It was not the greatest of pop magazines but her personal style and insider knowledge of the news behind the news made it essential reading. Penny was as much part of the scene as the people she interviewed. And I don't mean by that she was a groupie or someone who just hung around with the bands. Penny Valentine didn't copy press releases. She looked at the fast-changing Sixties fashions in music and wrote about them in depth. Penny was part of the Sixties team of creators, not a follower.

There was another very fine writer who made a name for herself at that time. Christine Bowler was tall with dark hair, beautiful long legs and pale grey-blue eyes. Christine freelanced but worked mainly for *Trend*, a better than most fan magazine. It was large format with an unfussy layout and imaginative use of pictures. She had no interest in being part of the so-called swinging scene. She lived happily with her cat not far from me in a basement flat in Crescent Grove.

Penny was full-on and non-stop in everything she did. She was excited by everything that presented itself as a new experience. Christine, on the other hand, kept her personal life a secret as she did with many of her thoughts. Penny didn't know what having a secret meant.

Penny came to interview me for *Disc* during the week of the launch of *AWSG*, in January 1966. It was bitterly cold that day. People headed to work in heavy coats and boots. Penny came dressed in a summer skirt and slingbacks. Not even a top coat. Just a scarf. She said it had turned out colder than she thought. I told her the flat only had a gas fire in the bedroom and a three-bar electric fire in the studio. I added that the only really warm place was my bed and she said that would do fine. Penny was petite and walked like a stripper, full of swing and bounce. What Eddie Carbone called 'walkin' wavy' in Arthur Miller's *A View from the Bridge*. She had the most wonderful slender neck, like something out of a Modigliani portrait and large pale cobalt eyes. Her hair was blonde and she sometimes kept it in a ponytail. Modigliani would have liked her as a model. He would have had fun with her wide lips and sensuous smile. A lot of fun. Because that is the way Penny lived her life.

Over the years we knew each other I discovered that we both had the same background. Her father was Italian and her mother Jewish. She came to the studio at the BBC each week when we did *AWSG* and came early. We'd spend an hour together in my dressing room. Penny would go over my lines with me because I was always very nervous. I had trained to be a painter, not a TV presenter. Those hours before the show were the best hours I ever spent with her.

When Penny edited *Disc* she asked me to do a weekly cartoon. She gave me a half page and said I could do what I wanted. In the fifty years I did cartoons, no other paper or magazine gave me that freedom. As time passed I saw less of Penny. We would meet for a drink now and then. Even when they are with you, talking to you, most people are busy planning the next move. Not Penny. She was one hundred per cent with you. All the time. And the pleasure she gave and the pleasure she took were all the richer for it. If there was a question about what came next I never heard her ask it. Nor did she go over what happened an hour ago. If she said she loved you, she said it not while wondering if the red Biba dress she'd bought that afternoon was the right shade. Love you meant love you. There and then.

Penny went on to work for *Time Out* and help found its more radical offshoot, *City Limits*. Never out of the limelight, Penny enjoyed stints appearing on the telly and making sure she lived each day as if it were her last. She died in 2003 after a long illness.

Christine was the total opposite of Penny. She hid from the limelight. Distrusted its distortions. Our time spent together was late at night, especially in summer. She'd stroll from her flat to my studio and we would drink cold white wine and create fantasy worlds. If Penny lived for the minute, Christine lived in dreams. She eventually married and had a daughter.

Then she divorced and now lives alone writing beautiful dreamlike stories for adults and children.

When I told her I was writing a book about the time we met she sent me a copy of the interview she wrote for *Trend* magazine in October 1966. As a cut-down version of my life at the time it comes pretty close. Sixties to the core – the writing and the subject.

You'll find him in his own special world overlooking Clapham Common. Wearing a baggy pair of jeans and a T-shirt with Superman printed on it. There he'll be planning out his next brushstroke on a canvas, or thinking up a new line for a song, or working out the way he's going to make a joke on televsion – answering the phone or putting on the whistling kettle that no longer whistles.

Busy, he always has time to say something funny, and friends he has many.

He has emerged to create a place for himself where there's humour and bright colours, and he likes to share it. He never misses a dolly who happens to be passing by his window, so he finds concentration a problem.

'There's this dolly outside the window,' he'll tell you over the phone. 'She's wearing a yellow plastic mac and has blonde hair. The rain's pouring down in buckets and it's dead sexy.'

'This bloke, a bus conductor, came up to me the other day,' he'll say. 'He stuck a piece of paper in front of my face. "Sign!" he ordered. He wanted an autograph for his daughter!'

He gets into his white saloon car, puts on a pair of those little square rimmed sunglasses and glides away.

He'll probably have only got to the other side of the Common when someone'll be honking him from behind because he's taking his time.

Hoot! Hoot! Hoot! from behind, and out of the car jumps Barry to see what's bugging the man behind who's driving his wife nowhere in a Mini.

After angry words Barry marches back to his car – an extraordinary figure to say the least – with the final cutting phrase: 'What must your wife think of you?'

'Get your 'aircut, mate!' floats through the air.

'That's a sure sign of defeat,' says Barry, settling himself back at the wheel. 'In these days of long-haired men how can you possibly yell that out as a form of abuse?'

Barry's ambition is to simply give people pleasure. He is sincere and genuine, and vulnerable because of it, and sometimes so enthusiastic about a thing that his words run away with him, or he can't manage to say what he wants to.

He woke up one morning and listened to 'Eleanor Rigby' and it moved him so much he cried. He is forever singing the praises of Paul McCartney's 'velvet' voice. 'The only person who can sometimes move me like that, when he sings, is Ray.' He has been mates with Ray Davies of the Kinks for years and years.

His flat, which he describes as spartan, consists of a big studio full of paintbrushes, oils, an old organ, a piano and a battered radiogram – and a living room that is without curtains or easy chairs and is dominated by a double bed covered by a flag bedspread. He loves flags because of the way they are designed.

Sometimes he picks up one of his guitars and strums away and sings a song, often funny. One of his latest compositions is called 'The Spanish Lady', about a boy who makes a date with a girl and goes to pick her up at home. Her mum shows him into the front room which is contemporary and tasteless. As he waits for her to get ready he realises that the only beautiful thing there is a Spanish lady dancing on the mantelpiece. When eventually she says she's ready, he jumps out of the front-room window, leaving his heart with the Spanish lady!

Although he's a painter, he hates the countryside, but he'll stop to marvel at a bird taking flight like a miniature aeroplane as he strolls over the Common, which he says 'is not like it used to be'.

When he gets depressed it hits him hard. When he received the news from the *Melody Maker* of his award as Top Male TV Artiste of the Year, it came just in time to bring him out of a black spell.

His next couple of days, spent at the studios doing a bit part, as himself, in the new Dudley Moore film *30 Is a Dangerous Age Cynthia!* were elated ones. Another film, *Just Like A Woman*, in which he plays a pop star is currently around.

He's working on a new James Bond-type character for Warner Brothers. He judges contests in places like Barking . . . and loves dolly birds above all. 'I have to be emotionally secure to work properly,' he says.

And there are many facets to the sensitive Mr Fantoni.

I cringe now reading the way Christine summed me up as a child of the Sixties but what she wrote was true. All of it. I would like to think that I have changed for the better. Grown up. But I fear that I have just grown old.

When I think about Penny and Christine now, I see them as two very different young women who had one very important thing in common. A very Sixties thing. Both took complete control of their own lives. They did what they wanted when they wanted. Chose who they loved and who they didn't. The pill had given many young women sexual freedom but the freedom that Penny and Christine enjoyed was only partially to do with who they slept with. It was the freedom to explore the fast-changing world around them. If the Sixties was a social revolution, then Christine Bowler and Penny Valentine led the revolt.

55

LITTLE MAN IN A LITTLE BOX

When you look at the top-selling records of the Sixties you will notice that a fair number of them were written by Lennon and McCartney. Or Ray. Or in some cases by Mick and Keith. This guaranteed that singers like Marianne, Peter and Gordon, Leapy Lee and Billy J. Kramer all got their singles into the charts. In many ways the songwriter was more important than the singer. It also helped if you got Paul to produce your record, as was the case with Mary Hopkin's 'Those Were The Days'. Paul also recorded Mary for the Apple label and she was one of the first artists he signed. Paul did not write 'Those Were The Days', though. It was a version of a Russian folk song from the Twenties that was first recorded by a long-forgotten Russian cabaret band. They are not credited on Mary's version. But that's the way it so often works. Writing a truly original song takes something close to genius. I have known one or two. But only one or two.

Paul did his best to make Mary a major star. He wrote her next single, 'Goodbye', but it didn't work out. Mary, the Welsh-speaking former folk singer from the Valleys, was to be little more than a two-hit wonder.

A couple of weeks after signing up with Peter Eden and Geoff Stephens they told me the time had come for me to record a single. Geoff thought I might like to record one of his songs, which would, given his long list of hits, almost certainly make the charts. He said he had written a song for me about a guy who misses his train and loses his girl and sleeps it off on a bench at Waterloo Station. I quite liked the tune and the lyric was in the right direction (not too adolescent) so I recorded it with another of Geoff's songs as the B-side called 'Diana Goodbye'. After hearing the playback it was clear that Geoff's style of writing didn't match my voice. I then suggested that I record one of my own songs, but I had no name as a songwriter and even less as a singer.

In the days that followed the redundant recording I argued in favour of recording my own material. I had written a hit for Marianne after all. But one hit was not enough. Geoff and Pete were adamant. They insisted that what I needed was a well-established writer. The bigger the name, the bigger the chance of making the charts. I suggested asking Ray if he would write something. We fixed up a meeting at the office. Ray said he had an idea for a song based on my being on television and had already started working on it. The title was 'Little Man In A Little Box'. When we had finished fixing the session dates we chatted for a while about songwriting.

Ray knew Geoff's work and told Geoff that songwriting had moved on from 'The Crying Game'. He said that a songwriter was now free to write about all kinds of subjects. Half joking, Ray told Geoff that you could even write a song about a brick wall. Geoff listened carefully. A week later Geoff came to the office and said he had written a song on the train. He lived out of town and to get in he took the line which passed through Winchester. He had noted that the cathedral was a prominent feature. He took a piece of crumpled paper out of his pocket and pressed it flat on the desk. 'It's called "Winchester Cathedral",' he said and then sang the first few lines, beating time with his fingers on the desk.

'Winchester Cathedral, you're bringing me down. You stood and you watched, as my baby left town.'

Pete and I looked at each other. It was hardly 'Waterloo Sunset'. Was Geoff having a joke? No. Geoff was not having a joke. Geoff put together a bunch of studio musicians and called them the New Vaudeville Band. He dressed them in Twenties blazers and straw hats and went on to make millions. His song became a novelty classic and was recorded by just about everyone. I was in the office the day Frank Sinatra called and said it would be his next single. Geoff currently lives in Switzerland. As far as I know he no longer writes songs about jilted lovers or a cathedral with the longest gothic nave in Europe.

We recorded 'Little Man In A Little Box' at Pye's studio, where the Kinks recorded. Ray produced the single, which had 'Fat Man' on the B-side. 'Fat Man' was inspired by Willie Rushton's drawings of fat men. He drew a lot of fat men, which may or may not have been unconscious references to himself. Instead of an electric bass, which was standard at the time and still is, I decided to use a tuba. I had grown up listening to Danny Kaye singing 'Tubby The Tuba' on the radio – it was very popular – and since my song was about a fat man, I got a tuba player to play the plodding bassline. The player was hired from an army band and he had never played any kind of pop music. This made his contribution even more effective as the sound I wanted had less to do with pop and more to do with pastiche. 'Little Man In A Little Box' got to about number 20 in the chart but didn't do as well as we had all hoped. Unfortunately it was released in the summer at the same time as the Troggs released 'Wild Thing'. They got all the air play and were on their way to being the next big thing.

While writing this memoir Ace Records released a compilation album of cover versions and other material written by Ray. 'Little Man In A Little Box' is featured and a few days ago I got my first royalty cheque for a record in fifty years. Thirty-three pence. I can't help thinking of a gag Jimmy Wheeler used to tell about a life insurance salesman selling a ninety-nine-year-old woman a policy. The punchline goes: 'Think of it this way, lady. You only pay a penny a week but it's a start.'

The first pressing of 'Little Man In A Little Box' is now a collectors' item and changes hands for ten times the original price. 'Fat Man', so I am told, is a disco hit in Manchester.

56

EYE GIRLS

I did a lot of jobs to help pay the rent before my exhibition at the Woodstock Gallery in 1963. I had been a lifeguard, a short-order chef, a tailor's assistant and a bookie's runner. I had bought and sold banned books such as *Lady Chatterley's Lover* and *The Naked Lunch* to Soho bookshops. I painted murals of Venice in Italian barber shops during the day and packed bread through the night at the RACS on Brixton Hill. But I had never worked in an office. Not any kind of office anywere. I had been in them, lots of them, but only to fill in forms or sign something.

Before I got my job at the *Eye* I imagined the place full of funny people telling jokes all day and satirists and wits from all over popping in with their latest material. There was a bit of that but not a lot. As the weeks went by I discovered that *Private Eye*'s office was just as ordinary, and often as dull, as any other set of rooms with a couple of desks, kettle, sink, filing cabinets, phones and pretty young girls to answer them. But the *Eye* girls were anything but standard office issue. They were not recruited from the local temp agency.

Eye girls in the first year of publication were all from upper-class families. It was a closed shop that was forced to open its doors to all over the years. The upper-class debs without the ability to type faster than a word a minute or stick a stamp on an envelope the right way up all got married and moved on. There was an urgent need for proper office girls.

The first to fill the gap was Gill Brooke. With her northern background and hard-working parents who lived in a two-room flat in Ealing, Gill was anything but what Nancy Mitford (eldest daughter of the Hon. David Bertram Ogilvy Freeman-Mitford, later 2nd Baron Redesdale and a big fan of Adolf Hitler) called Non-U. Gill worked at the *Eye* for about three years. When Gill left she was replaced by Diana Clarke. Diana was middle-class, blonde, very beautiful, and quickly established herself as the office favourite. She lived in a small comfortable flat with another pretty girl of the same age who became a celebrity for a short while after winning the *Evening Standard* Dolly of the Year Competition.

Tony Rushton, Willie's cousin and layout man, was the first to become attached to Di, as she called herself. He took Di out. Took Di home. Cooked Di breakfast. Known as 'Tone', Rushton had served in the Marines and done a course in art history at the Courtauld. This clearly was enough to qualify him as the man to stick down the copy and then send it off to the printers. Tone was greatly influenced by the Bauhaus School of Design. Bauhaus designers went in for running type down the sides of pages and leaving large blank spaces. Tone insisted on trying to do the same with the layout of the *Eye* but Ingrams was quick to spot a large blank space. Even so, Tone would try it on, to Ingrams' great annoyance. 'Fucking Tone,' he would grunt as he tore into shreds yet another page full of blank spaces and type running along the edge and demand it be filled.

Tone was a bachelor and dressed in style. When I had my telly show, the Kinks had just released 'A Dedicated Follower Of Fashion'. We filmed Tone in Carnaby Street trying on gear to go with the music. Although affectionate and loving and open-minded, Di lacked the commitment needed for her job at the *Eye*. When a new girl took over from Di (it might have been Katie Jones), she found hundreds of applications and cheques for subs stuffed behind the filing cabinet. Thousands of pounds' worth. But her wicked sense of humour and ability to cruelly mimic even her dearest chums and bedfellows made up for the lost readers.

The cartoons waiting to be selected or rejected were kept in a large cardboard box which I got from the Vietnamese grocery shop on the ground floor. It had been used to store what were sold as 'hundred-year-old eggs', and from the smell of the box, my guess is they were not far out. The first thing you noticed on entering the editor's office was the smell of very old eggs. The couple who ran the grocery shop said very little and I never once saw them laugh until a motorcyclist drove into the wall of the theatre opposite our building. They could hardly stand up from laughing. They actually held their sides and wept.

In 1968 Paul Foot left the *Sunday Telegraph* to join the *Eye*. He brought his secretary with him. Tessa Reidy was a tall strikingly beautiful redhead with long legs and fierce green eyes who could do shorthand and touch type. But she was more than a secretary. Not long after Di left, Tessa took over running the office. She made a lot of changes. She had a knack for design and layout, which she used to great effect later in her life when she opened a number of shops selling her handbound books and stationery. Tessa quickly and effortlessly devised the first office filing system and built up a reference library which is still used to this day. Tessa also kept Ingrams' desk from collapsing under the weight of unread letters, yellowing back issues and submitted cartoons that still waited a 'Yes Please' or 'No Thanks' or 'Try *Punch*'. This she did by coming in twice a year with a black plastic sack and filling it with the entire desk top. And the desk drawers. And the stuff under the desk. The desk has not changed since issue six and Ian's treatment of it is not unlike Ingrams'. But he doesn't have a Tessa to sort it out.

(Tessa and I married on May Day, 1972, in St Mary's Church, a ten-minute walk from 60 South Side. On Paul Foot's advice we spent our honeymoon in Venice, staying in the Hotel Principe. Giant bathrooms and breakfast on the bank of the canal.)

57

NINETY MINUTES

From the moment England captain Bobby Moore lifted the World Cup on the afternoon of 30 July 1966, football suddenly became front-page news. Not just the England team. Or the cup. Football. It didn't matter who. Beatlemania took a temporary back seat as young men started playing football as well as guitars. All over the country, parks and grounds that had been more or less empty for decades were suddenly full of players eager to emulate Alf Ramsey's heroes. From my studio at 60 South Side I could see the dozen or so football pitches on the Common. Previously deserted on Sunday mornings, they were now filled with cobbled-together local teams.

I used to wander over and watch for a while. Cheer when someone scored and boo the ref when he got it wrong. Some players were clearly out of shape. They did more shouting than running but there were plenty who knew the game and how to play it. There was a very good side made up entirely of local Italian waiters and chefs. They wore the red-and-black strip of AC Milan and called themselves AC Balham. When I told Mario, the guy who organised the team, I was Italian, he asked me if I wanted to join them. I had played a lot of football growing up and got as far as being picked to play for South London Juniors. I agreed and turned out the following Sunday wearing number nine and scored twice in a two-all draw with the team from Young's Brewery.

It felt good kicking a ball again and I decided to form a team of my own. I knew Ray had been a player and was once on Arsenal's books as a teenager. Dave was also good. And Ian

La Frenais had mentioned playing a fair bit in Newcastle as a kid. We met and agreed to find some more players. Ian said Tom Courtenay played. It was like that bit in *The Magnificent Seven* when Chris is looking for gunmen to protect the village. So far we had Ray, Dave, Ian, Tom and me. We were six short.

This all took place around the time I was doing illustrations for the *Melody Maker*. Chris Welch, one of the key feature writers, wrote a weekly satire on the pop world called 'Jiving K Boots'. I was in the office delivering artwork one day when I got talking to the production manager Bill. He was thinking about starting an office football team and asked me if I played. He was short of five players. I told him I had five, and at once we were 'The Magnificent Eleven'. But you can't call a football team 'The Magnificent Eleven'. Maybe Brazil or Italy, but not us.

When jazz was the thing, *MM* recorded the annual poll-winners for Esquire Records and it was a big event. The band was called the Melody Maker All-Stars so we used the name. Some who played remember it differently. Dave thinks we called ourselves the Melody Maker Eleven. But no matter, the combined squad of performers and *MM* staff played a whole season. Our opponents were teams who, like ours, were created from scratch and not in a position to join a league with a proper fixture list. Our games were arranged on a casual basis. Most of the sides we played were of a similar standard. Mid-table teams who won just a few more than they lost. The game against the Tax Office proved to be the most satisfying victory (3–2). At least for the high earners. For them it was personal – a form of revenge.

(In 1966 Wilson had hiked tax up to 83 per cent for people in the top bracket: Ray, Dave, Ian and Tom. And it was to get worse. In a few years it was to hit 98 per cent. As one Rolling Stone put it at the time, 'If I earn a million quid, I only bank seventy thousand. No point, mate, living here.' And he, along with the other members of 'The World's Greatest Rock and Roll Band' took off for France.)

The match was also memorable for an incident in the second half. Dave was through and about to take a shot at goal when the overweight Tax Office's centre-half intervened. 'Get out the way, fatty,' was Dave's memorable remark. Fatty refused and Dave bulldozed him to the ground in order to find the net. If there was a way to sum up Dave Davies, I would say this was it. Arrogance, skill and not a little good fortune. When Ray talks about 'the fatty incident', with just a touch of the often exaggerated sibling discord, he seldom misses the opportunity to point out that due to Dave's life of excess, he now bears more than a passing resemblance to the Tax Office's seventeen-stone centre-half.

When the *MM* team folded a year later I joined the *Sunday Times* Eleven and then got picked for the Show Biz squad, who played charity matches all over the UK. The most enjoyable by far was a game we played at the Molineux stadium, home of Wolverhampton Wanderers FC. To make the fixture attractive and not too one-sided, the organisers decided to mix up the teams. The Show Biz Eleven would be merged with former Wolves stars, who would play a combination of first and reserve team players. I was given the number eight shirt, which in those days meant playing inside right. The centre-half was one of England's greatest defenders, Billy Wright, a player who even today holds the record for an unbroken run of appearances at international level. On his left was Ron Flowers, another great passer of the ball. The difference between playing with professionals and anyone else is that when a professional passes you the ball, it arrives at your feet. At all other times you have to chase it. Pros do not run around chasing the ball. They stroll. Throughout the whole ninety minutes I could hear a voice behind me saying, 'Here you are, Barry,' and the ball would be on my toe. I'd turn my head quickly to see Billy or Ron smiling. I have never enjoyed a game more.

That Sunday afternoon in the Midlands, the two teams raised £3,000 for research into spina bifida. On the coach back to London, I couldn't stop myself feeling a growing resentment that medical research should not be funded by coins thrown into a tin cup on the high street. Or a football match. It should never be forced to rely on an act of charity. Where was the money the government took in taxes? What was it being spent on? Obviously not on finding ways to cure the deformed spines of babies. Not then, not now.

58

THE WRONG SIDE OF THE DESK

When Peter Cook came to the joke sessions at the *Eye*, the hierarchy of the seating changed because there were only three proper chairs and there were four people. Booker, Ingrams, Cook and me. Cook sat on my chair so, being the youngest and not having been to public school, I was relegated to the Fifties adjustable swivel chair that was neither adjustable nor swivellable and frequently collapsed as soon as you sat on it. This meant I perched on the edge of the desk I used to draw cartoons. Cook didn't actually sit on my chair. He perched on the back support and put his feet on the seat while balancing his briefcase with its supply of fags and booze on his knees.

Peter kept his bottle of spirits wrapped in a bag, as if he didn't want us to know he was drinking. We went along with him and never mentioned it. We all agreed that when Cook was there, by just being there, the jokes were funnier.

Peter's mind worked in a different way to the rest of us. Deep down, I think we all aspired to be as funny as Cook but it was impossible. We did what we knew and what we were good at. And we were all prepared to be judged on our limitations. But even so, there would be a time when one of the team would make a gag that would get a big laugh and then someone would say 'Cook'. Meaning the gag was as good as if it were Peter's.

When we first met, Peter's life was an ever-expanding success story. Greatly gifted. Handsome. Confident. There seemed no end to what Peter was capable of achieving. The downturn came from Peter attempting to take on challenges that were not his thing. For reasons I could never fully understand Peter decided to become a TV interviewer. It was a disaster.

Peter was not interested in dull showbiz types and it quickly became apparent that he was sitting on the wrong side of the desk. Peter got panned for the first time in his life and it stung him. He began drinking. And when the *Daily Mail* hired him to write a column it was another mistake. Peter was a performer. His genius lay not simply in the words but the way they were presented. All his jokes came off the top of his head. Writing a column for a newspaper is a slog at best. It gets subbed and changed, and if it is the *Daily Mail* you won't get much space for poking fun at the four million bigots* who read it. The hacks who write for the *Daily Mail* are just doing a well-paid job to appease millions of right-wing nutters.

Again, Peter got stick for his efforts. Unfairly. They were not really all that bad. A bit wordy and a little flat at times, but more entertaining by a mile than anything else you read in the *Mail*, before or since. ('Flook', a brilliant comic strip written by George Melly and illustrated by cartoonist Trog – Wally Fawkes – that ran daily until the rag became a Tory Party mouthpiece, was the one exception.)

The effect of two failures in a row caused Peter to drink a lot more. He became more reclusive. Then he made *Bedazzled* with Dudley. It was to be a Big Statement. To silence his critics. But *Bedazzled* did not do as well as Peter hoped. The film just about covered its costs, and although the reviews were generally favourable and it had seven minutes of Raquel Welch to help keep cinema audiences amused, there was

---

* *Collins Dictionary* describes a bigot as a person who is intolerant of any ideas other than his or her own, especially on religion, politics or race.

nevertheless the feeling of a very mild flop about it. *Bedazzled* had its moments – enough to inspire a dreadful remake in 2000 – but there were not enough of them. It was a step backwards.

I met Dudley less often than Peter because he never came to the *Eye* unless it was to take part in a recording. Dudley played piano with his trio at the Establishment Club in the early Sixties and I sometimes asked to sit in, playing alto. The *Eye*'s office was next door. Cook owned the leases of both. Dudley came from a working-class background. He was born in Dagenham. But his name didn't sound working-class and his accent was even posher than Pete's.

Over the years many have tried to suggest there was bad blood between Peter and Dudley. It is true that Peter could never quite take Dudley's Hollywood persona seriously but that hardly constitutes ill-feeling. The last time I saw Peter and Dudley together was at a small birthday party that Peter had arranged for Dudley. The guest list that night at the White House, an Italian restaurant in Hampstead, consisted of Dud and his wife, Peter and his wife, a very nice man who worked in advertising, Stephen Fry and Mr and Mrs Fantoni. It was clear that Dudley was not well and he hardly said a thing all night. Peter never sat down. He spent the entire evening making sure Dudley was comfortable and had everything he wanted.

The truth is that there are some relationships, especially those involving people who are highly creative – and in the case of Peter Cook, a genius – where emotions and deep feelings rise quickly to the surface. Things are said that are not really meant. Pete and Dud had their differences, it is true. But not often, and they never threatened their relationship.

More important than the odd professional tiff was the very great bond that existed between them. In a sense Pete and Dud (later Derek and Clive) were two parts of the whole. Like all great comic teams. But you had to be close to one or both of them to know it for certain.

Peter divorced his first wife Wendy in 1971. He then married and divorced deb/model Judy Huxtable. He then married Lin Chong, who he met at the Playboy Club. They lived in separate homes. Dudley married and divorced Suzy Kendall, Tuesday Weld, Brogan Lane and Nicole Rothschild. My reasoning is that when two men are married to each other, as were Pete and Dud, you don't have a lot of time for partners. Some double acts could do both. Morecambe and Wise made a go of it. Laurel and Hardy didn't. Neither did Pete and Dud.

Peter was fifty-seven when he died from internal bleeding caused by his heavy drinking and nicotine addiction. It was one of the most bitter days of my life. I wrote his obituary for the *Guardian* the day after he died. It was Press Monday at the *Eye*, and as soon as we'd put the magazine to bed I went to their offices in Farringdon and used one of their computers to compose my thoughts. I referred to the cartoon that Peter and I did which was our most popular collaboration. It goes like this. Two men are talking. One says to the other, 'I am writing a book.' The other replies, 'Neither am I.'

One of the last conversations we had was about Peter's mother. She was over ninety and had recently lost her eyesight. I asked him if she could still drive as I knew she lived some distance from the centre of town. He said, 'She does. Mostly into other cars.'

59

GONKS

I began studying at Camberwell a few months after my fifteenth birthday. It was the policy then to teach art at an early age. No other qualifications were required other than the ability to draw and paint well above what was considered the average. After two years in the Junior Department, which provided lessons on puppetmaking and a couple of hours a week doing rudimentary maths and English (required by the 1944 Education Act), twenty teenage students had the option of moving on to the Senior School. There, they would study painting or sculpture or one of the two main crafts. These were ceramics and fabric design. Or they were free to leave and find a job. Most stayed on.

Only one student I knew, who decided to leave before completing the course, did anything more than fade into the world of nine-to-five. We had a drink together the day he left in 1955. Over a pint of cider he told me that he came from a big family and I think he said his father was a bus driver. In any event, they were always short of money. He told me he was going to leave and find a way of making some. 'I've got a few ideas,' he said. 'I'm good at puppetmaking. Maybe I can do something with puppets.'

Bob left just before the summer term and I neither heard of him nor saw him again until the spring of 1961. Del Shannon's 'Hats Off To Larry' was number one. I was strolling down Carnaby Street when I saw Bob getting out of a Rolls-Royce. The hit song was coming from his car radio. I had not expected to see him again. And especially not getting out of a Rolls.

Even as a junior student, Bob always kept himself looking smart. His style was more Teddy Boy than Paris Bohemian. He wore his hair in a DA and spent what little cash he had on a suit with a velvet collar and long drape. Well dressed. That was Bob as a fifteen-year-old.

Now, he was wearing an expensive dark blue mohair suit, obviously tailor-made, Italian shoes, an Italian silk tie and an Ivy League shirt. Arrow made them. They had a collar pin that ran under the knot in the tie and they were the most expensive off-the-peg shirts you could buy. It came with a choice of arm lengths and shoulder widths and was made from the finest American cotton. Bob's hair was cut and blow-dried in the style of teen idol Billy Fury. He saw me and came over.

'Hello, Bal,' he said. 'How do you like the Roller?'

'Are you going to a wedding?' I asked.

He lit an American cigarette with a gold-plated lighter. 'The Rolls is mine. Paid for. Cash,' he said and pointed to Liberty's window. It was full of egg-shaped furry animals with big eyes. 'I've invented the Gonk.'

Bob could see I had no idea what he was talking about. Or what I was looking at in Liberty's window.

'Gonks,' he explained. 'They're all the craze. Mammoth. Kids. Housewives. Everyone loves Gonks. I thought them up myself and my girlfriend got busy with the sewing machine. We made a handful to kick off with and then we started selling them in the market on Saturday, and a bloke came up who said he was a buyer for Liberty's and said he'd take a dozen to show people there, and then we got an order from Liberty's. And then all the other big shops came along and I've got a bloody great factory out in Kent full of girls making them seven days a week. We turn out thousands a day and next year they're going to make a film called *Gonks Go Beat*. I tell you, even the Yanks want a slice. No kidding. I'm a fucking millionaire.'

If you wanted the story of Swinging London in a nutshell, you need look no further than Gonks. Hats off to Bob.

60

VILLAGE LIFE

In the very early days of the Sixties, Soho was still like a village. In fact, a lot of places in London were like villages; some still are. Highgate is an example. Clapham was, and is now, considered a village. I suppose you could say that boroughs are very similar to villages, certainly the older London boroughs such as Stepney and several others that line the Thames. Soho village was made up of quarters that were Italian, French, German and one which was a mix of Chinese and people who were known as Bohemians. These were mainly painters and writers who found the cheap rents and centrality of the area good reasons to live there. And there was the French House, a freehouse where the Bohemians hung out.

'The French' as it was known by its motley clientele was strictly for heavy drinkers, and Gaston, the large Frenchman with a handlebar moustache who owned the place, was very picky about who he served. He liked actors, painters, poets and criminals. One villain, known as Jack Spot, was shot dead outside one Sunday morning. A drunken Dylan Thomas left his only copy of *Under Milk Wood* on the table of the French one night, to find it was still there on the table when his BBC radio producer went back for it the next day. Quentin Crisp spent many happy and adventurous hours there with young men in naval uniform.

Although there can be no doubt that the Sixties Revolution began in Soho, there is some doubt as to exactly when it began. There are differing opinions. It was certainly not 1 January 1960. It is not possible to be that accurate. It is not a date you can fix, like the beginning of the millennium. Or the day war broke out. It was fluid. A process. Like the French Revolution or the Italian Renaissance. My view is that the Sixties began in Soho in the mid-to late Fifties.

It took root in the coffee bars on Old Compton Street where skiffle music was fast gaining a following that was not interested in the Shadows' clean-cut look and tepid dance routines. This audience saw in skiffle music, and its gradual evolution into early rock and roll, something closer to the world of art and culture. Those who played skiffle and those who listened were mainly art students. It is a fact. Virtually all the key players of the Sixties Revolution had been to art schools and colleges. They were not interested in Cliff singing 'Bachelor Boy'. Rock and roll was where it was at. The way forward. The sign of the times and the universal expression of a reaction to the grey, dismal, dead-end postwar years.

The very late Fifties saw the emergence of music that was not a pale copy of an American hit but home-grown. The roots were American but that was all. No matter how hard they tried to make it sound American, British bands had a sound of their own. Less swing. Less commercial. And better for it. The end of the decade was when Felicity Innes made her first mini skirt and Mary Quant had the good sense to take it to another level. It was when an aging Vince Green fell in love with the young John Stephen and helped him redesign men's clothing. Carnaby Street is where it happened. Where Gear opened and Cranks had their first salad bar. In Soho. Where, in Covent Garden, Felicity got her black tights from the ballet suppliers, Anello & Davide. From the same shop the Beatles got their Cuban heels. Shoes used to dance the Flamenco. Soho was where you bought an electric guitar or found a basement to rehearse in. Where you met other musicians. And if you crossed Regent Street you would find a dozen small art galleries willing to show new work. All in all, there were about a hundred or so people who made the Sixties what it was.

Politics played a minor role. Once the satire boom was over, the only time you saw a politician mentioned was when they were having affairs with call girls or giving the Beatles a gong.

By late 1968 Swinging London was over. The decade of pop and fashion gave way to the demo and unrest. The Red Brigade. The Munich Olympics. The bombs of the IRA. Riots. It was to become an age where I could find no common ground with those who had made it their own. As the Seventies gradually took hold I was increasingly aware that the world I had been so much a part of had moved on. It was time for me to do the same.

PRIVATE VIEW

ACKNOWLEDGEMENTS

Thanks to Neville Moir, Alison Rae and everyone at Polygon Books, photographer Eric Hands and designer Teresa Monachino.

BARRY FANTONI
Nude Reclining
1963
Oil on hardboard 152 x 122 cm
Private collection

This is the painting that infamously hoaxed the Royal Academy
Summer Show in 1963. I painted it under the name of Stuart
Harris and did not reveal that it was my work until the very last
day. The RA had never shown a Pop Art painting before and it
caused a sensation. The press spent the summer trying to locate
the nonexistent Harris. The *Mirror* was convinced it was painted
by David Frost, mainly because I sent them an anonymous tip-off
suggesting it. I bought the porn mag that the judge is holding
(which is why the painting is called *Nude Reclining*) from a shop
in Soho. For the foreground, I filled a table with objects that were
lying around the studio. The cake was a leftover from my recent
twenty-third birthday and I still have the bottle of Camp coffee.
The label illustration of a soldier in a kilt sitting outside a tent in
India drinking ersatz coffee while being attended to by a servant in
a turban is priceless. My painting, which I also consider priceless,
vanished in 1964, only to resurface earlier this year.

BARRY FANTONI
Brockwell Park Lido
1961
Oil on canvas 63 x 51 cm
Artist's collection

I made a lot of new friends working as a lifeguard at the lido. I
fell in love with one. She is in the centre of the painting wearing a
yellow bikini. Inge was from Austria and worked as an au pair for
a wealthy and successful lawyer called Bill Fournier. I offered to
marry Inge at one point but when I finally got to meet her father,
he took one look at me and that was that. No Jews. He was serious.
Bill was to become my first patron and the little girl holding Inge's
hand is his daughter, Louise. She now lives in Richmond where her
father's large collection hangs intact on the walls of her splendid
Victorian house. The young man in the black trunks behind Inge
with the red beard is Chris Gosden. I rented a room cum studio
in his flat at that time. An Oxford graduate, Chris later went on
to teach the Prime Minister of Portugal English. I put myself in,
hands on hips, under a lad diving from the top board.